PERFORMANCE PSYCHOLOGY FOR DANCERS

PERFORMANCE PSYCHOLOGY FOR DANCERS

ERIN SANCHEZ, DAVE COLLINS AND
ÁINE MACNAMARA

THE CROWOOD PRESS

First published in 2021 by
The Crowood Press Ltd
Ramsbury, Marlborough
Wiltshire SN8 2HR

enquiries@crowood.com

www.crowood.com

© Erin Sanchez, Dave Collins and Áine MacNamara 2021

All rights reserved. No part of this publication may be reproduced or transmitted in any form or by any means, electronic or mechanical, including photocopy, recording, or any information storage and retrieval system, without permission in writing from the publishers.

British Library Cataloguing-in-Publication Data
A catalogue record for this book is available from the British Library.

ISBN 978 1 78500 798 9

Photography © Dani Bower Photography 2020. Company: Motionhouse

Dancers: Alasdair Stewart, Bryn Aled, Beth Pattison, Chris Knight, Elly Welford, Junior Cunningham and Sophie Page

Cover: Dancers take physical and psychological risks, but when navigated and supported with appropriate psychological skills, success can be achieved even in very challenging environments.

Frontispiece: Doubt isn't necessarily a sign of failure, but perhaps more often an indication of the strength of intention and meaning brought to the challenge.

Typeset by Simon and Sons

Cover design by Maggie Mellett

Printed and bound in India by Replika Press Pvt Ltd

CONTENTS

Dedication	6
Preface	7
Acknowledgements	8
Introduction	11
Part I: Ideas	17
1 Parameterizing the Challenge: Which Way is *The* Way?	19
Part II: Tools	33
2 Introduction to Psychological Characteristics of Developing Excellence	35
3 Meeting the Psychomotor Demands of Dance	55
4 Talent Development Environments for Dance	71
5 Parenting and Supporting the Performer – Mental Challenges Along the Pathway	87
Part III: Realities	101
6 Pitfalls and Challenges	103
Part IV: Action	119
7 Where Next: Future Steps and Sources of Information	121
Bibliography	129
About the Authors	138
Photo Index	140
Index	141

DEDICATION

Áine MacNamara

To Damian, Síofra and Iarlaith for their support.

Dave Collins

For Helen, Joe, Judy, Rosie, Ruby and Lily... my own personal 'lead me a merry dance' company.

Erin Sanchez

To my family, Sanchez, Mills, Baca, Cordova, Garcia, Cooley, Taggart, Harley, Ansell, Wyon, Matt, Laura, Lara, Sarah, Mark, Will, Josh, Renee, ABKB, and Penni, for teaching me to be kind and love people and to steer into fear. With you, life is rich.

PREFACE

The book you hold in your hands is a product of (at this point) decades of focused academic research and clinical and applied work by Prof. Dave Collins and Prof. Áine MacNamara in talent development and psychological skills, as well roughly nine years of my own interest and work in supporting dancers' health.

The book began when Dave was approached to write about dance talent development and psychological skills. I was lucky enough to be the person he asked to collaborate with him, alongside Prof. Áine MacNamara. After nearly three years (and many panics on my part), we have created this book.

For me, this book has been an enormous challenge and source of fear and anxiety. How could one book be the answer to the many challenges dancers will face during their training? How could we ensure that the book provided the most evidence-based and best guidance, for everyone? How could we make sure that every person that engaged in dance had a positive experience?

I learnt an enormous lesson during this process – no book can do things like that. No one piece of advice or single source of knowledge – whether it be a book, a person, a method or style of training – will give dancers everything they need to become successful. Every pathway to success will require a different combination of support and challenge. The advice in this book may not apply to you, or it may be useful guidance for you at some times and not at others, or it just may be a very helpful tool and once it is used, you need to move on to another tool to keep growing and developing. I hope it will be clear that our aim is to provide questions to consider, principles to use, and confidence to apply them to your particular goals and challenges.

I'm a perfectionist. In my life, that has sometimes driven me to work hard and look for ways to improve. At other times, it has made me question myself and my abilities, and to forget my accomplishments and only see my failures. At times in my life, wanting to be perfect has made me want to give up. I'm still learning to embrace both sides: first, to see that doubt isn't necessarily a sign of failure but perhaps, more often, an indication of the strength of intention and meaning brought to the challenge; and, second, to recognize that striving for high standards can be a superpower, providing energy and strength to achieve challenging things. And every (scary, self-doubt inducing) challenge is a chance to grow.

We sincerely hope that this book is something that can be useful to you. As you, and we, gain new knowledge, there will likely be more editions of this book to add to the conversation.

Erin Sanchez

ACKNOWLEDGEMENTS

We want to acknowledge the people who have contributed to the creation of this book.

Photographs: to Dani Bower who captured the beauty, strength, and fearlessness of dancers Alasdair Stewart, Berta Contijoch, Beth Pattison, Bryn Aled, Chris Knight, Elly Welford, Junior Cunningham and Sophie Page of Motionhouse for the gorgeous images used in this book. We are grateful to them for sharing their craft.

Thank you also to incredible photographer Danilo Moroni, who assisted with the first discussions about the book and, although in the end we couldn't find the right time to have a shot for this book, his beautiful work will certainly be included in the next edition.

Experts: we are immensely grateful to the experts who provided guidance and feedback, as well as expert commentaries, for selected chapters. They include Elsa Urmston, Fuschia Peters, Jodie Clark, Kathleen McGuire Gaines, Khyle Eccles, Stephanie De'Ath and Tala Lee Turton. Thank you for all the conversations over coffee or by email, and thank you most of all for the inspiration and support you give every day – you are changing the lives of young dancers.

Dave Collins

So pleased to have the privilege of contributing to performers who have enormously more skill than I could ever muster.

Erin Sanchez

Many thanks also go to Anastasia Paschali and Emma Turner, who contributed to the creation of this book by gathering information, distilling ideas and generally connecting the dots where needed.

The international field of dance medicine and science includes an exceptionally welcoming, familial and passionate group of professionals. Thank you to the International Association for Dance Medicine and Science for hosting their annual conference to allow us to meet and exchange, in what can sometimes feel a very isolated professional environment.

There is also a community of experts whose indirect impact through publications, presentations, collaborative activities and works of art made this book possible. Each of them in their own lives has contributed a great deal to the conversation about dance talent development, professional success, dance psychology, mental health, and lived experience of mental illness in dance. We commend them for their selfless and powerful work:

Joey Chua; Sara Ascenso; Lynda Mainwaring; Prof Paula Thomson; Bonnie Robson; Janet Karin; Dr Liliana Araújo; Vicki Balaam; Stuart Waters; Steve Peck; Sarah Maguire; Colin Bland; Hannah Friebel; Natalia Atkins; Caldonia Walton; Jaimie Tapper; Prof Jon Arcelus; Rae Bonney; Kym King; Rachel Bar; Dr Monique Faleafa; Brendon Hansford; James Williams; Omari Carter; Tomorr

ACKNOWLEDGEMENTS

Kokona; Wendy Reinert; Kevin Turner; Helen Linsell; Mark Archer; Phaedra Petsilas; Megan Preston; Gemma Fuller; Debbie Malina; Dancers Career Development; Dance Professionals Fund; Nicoletta P Lekka; Allan Johnston; Alan Currie; Dr Phil Hopley; Dr Tim Rogers; Dr Huw Goodwin; Dr Irina Roncaglia; Prof Gene Moyle.

I personally have been lucky to share a common aim, language and set of very ambitious goals with five inspiring, creative, passionate people in my work over the past ten years. To Helen Laws, Claire Farmer, Stephanie De'Ath, Sarah Needham-Beck and Niamh Morrin – whose work ethic, passion and commitment cannot be overstated.

I am also indebted to Sanna Nordin Bates, Imogen Aujla, Prof. Emma Redding, Lucie Clements, Jennifer Cumming, Dr Klara Edlund, Siobhan Mitchell, and Charlotte Downing for giving me the courage, and the encouragement, to write.

Finally, to my family, some of whom are blood (Sanchez, Baca, Cordova, Garcia, Cooley Taggart, Harley, Mills and Wyon) and some of whom may as well be (Laura, Lara, Will, Josh, Renee and the Ansells), and to whom I owe, literally, everything.

The content of the book covers how aspiring dancers may develop their goals and, ultimately, define what success means to them. A toolbox of strategies is drawn from selected literature, including our own, to apply to talent development pathways; exemplar experiences of excellent performers; and a planning section to plot actions based on evidence and trustworthy advice.

INTRODUCTION

The International Association for Dance Medicine and Science was formed in 1990 when a groundswell of researchers, educators and clinicians came together with the aim to enhance the well-being and performance of dancers through medicine, research and education. Over the past thirty years, thousands of papers have been published in this domain (Solomon & Solomon, 2014), educational programmes at bachelors, masters and PhD level have graduated hundreds of students, and several national organizations are devoted to specific work in this area. Despite this growth, very little of the research coming from this field is being implemented into training or performing practice (cf. Collins, MacNamara & Cruickshank, 2018). One key area in need of further evidence-informed practice is training and talent development, which is essential in a competitive and demanding career pathway.

Why Psychological Skills Matter: The Challenges

Research indicates that pre-professional or competitive dance training and professional careers are physically, psychologically and economically challenging and require robust preparation. Incidence of injury, as measured retrospectively and through clinical records, is historically and consistently high, at 74–80 per cent (e.g. Laws, 2005; Hincapie et al., 2008, 2012; Allen et al., 2014). Pain and injury affect dancers' employment, ability to earn, performance and career longevity (Tarr & Thomas, 2011), and injury treatment is rare given the incidence, possibly due to lack of available support, fear of injury severity or desire to continue dancing (Kerr et al., 1992; Mainwaring et al., 1993; Laws, 2005). Relative energy deficiency (formerly called the female athlete triad) is also a key concern for dancers. A combination of aesthetic, physiological and mechanical factors mean that a low weight confers an advantage in dance training and careers (Keay, 2018). Most dancers will not have the benefit of support from a dietician or strength and conditioning coach, and thus, efforts to control or change weight, or simply energy imbalance resulting from training load, can result in relative energy deficiency.

Although physical concerns are very serious, retrospective interviews in the UK have reported that, between 1993 and 2002, there was a reduced incidence of smoking and eating problems, reduced injuries due to environmental factors and ignoring early warning signs, and an increase in positive training factors, such as cooling down (Laws, 2005). This may be due to the gradual expansion of medical, physiological and nutritional support, especially within large ballet and contemporary companies and schools in the UK during this time. However, where these areas have grown, psychological support, education and interventions for mental health and psychological performance enhancement are still rare, with challenges

INTRODUCTION

such as drug and alcohol abuse and external stress increasing over time points. Notably, psychological problems were more common than injury, with 92 per cent of dancers reporting at least one concern in the past twelve months, and 85 per cent reporting more than one, including 41 per cent stating that they had experienced general anxiety (Laws, 2005). Dancers also report practical concerns that may predispose them to increased stress levels: that employment and income are uncertain, work schedules are erratic, careers in dance are often economically limited and unstable, competition for employment is high, and dancers regularly face a job market with too few vacancies for the available workers (Hamilton et al., 1989; Riley, 2016; Aujla, 2019).

Dance performance also lacks objective criteria for achievement. Quantitative and qualitative measures for dance performance exist in ballet and contemporary dance, including marks for technique, expressiveness, x-factor or overall performance/impressiveness above and beyond motor skill, coordination or accuracy (Angioi et al., 2009; Krasnow & Chatfield, 2009), but such measures are not used in formal talent identification or development processes. Aesthetic expectations in ballet are also evolving with time, requiring increased flexibility and strength (Daprati et al., 2009), but with no objective standard and little guidance on evidence-based and safe training practices, dancers often adopt an approach where more is always better. Subjective opinions of gatekeepers will determine success in securing training opportunities, employment, promotion and recognition. In many cases, poor communication or lack of transparency between the dancer and gatekeepers regarding all the above points can lead to experiences of self-doubt, low confidence, contingent self-worth and burnout (Turton, 2018).

Dance Education and Psychological Skills

Taken together, these many challenges demand a varied and well-developed physical and psychological skillset for a successful training and career in dance, and there are calls for dance education (talent development pathways) to respond (Jackson, 1996; Bennett, 2009; Risner, 2010).

Talent development in many full-time dance training environments represents the final developmental step before entrance into the profession. Evidence-based talent identification and development strategies are developing in dance, but have been a challenge to implement, partially due to a lack of structured understanding of constantly changing career demands, but also due to the lack of funding and time to implement evidence into practice. Educational practices, especially in vocational training, can be dictated by tradition. As indicated by the level of injury among dancers and the incidence of dropout in vocational training environments, discussed above, some traditional methods can result in situations where dancers survive rather than thrive, and where the emergence of dancing excellence is a rare occurrence rather than a planned and supported outcome. Creating optimal dance talent development environments is complex. Aujla and colleagues (2014) state, 'Specifically, literature reviews in both sport and dance indicate that optimal talent development depends upon a range of variables including student commitment, teacher behaviour, structured learning and practice, as well as physical facility, all of which educators can influence in the studio' (p.4).

Creating successful professional dancers has also historically been a challenge for talent pathways; in 2015, three critically acclaimed and financially successful contemporary dance choreographers in the UK jointly stated that the top three British contemporary dance

INTRODUCTION

conservatoires were not producing dancers of an employable standard. A similar concern has been voiced about the lack of British ballet dancers in the upper ranks of leading ballet companies in the UK (Eden, 2013). These concerns have touched off industry-wide debate about dance training in the UK. In the case of the contemporary dance sector, this centred on defining the demands of a professional's career in contemporary dance – namely, that career pathways were diverse and successful training of graduates cannot only be measured on performance quality alone. Judith Mackrell, dance critic for *The Guardian* wrote:

> If we're going to debate whether our training institutions are fit for purpose, we have to consider exactly what that purpose is… not simply in terms of training the 'best' performers in the world, or honing the most beautiful bodies – Rather, it's to offer the widest, most creative kind of dance education possible.
>
> The philosophy of the UK's top institutions is that the dance industry is about far more than performance.
> *(Mackrell, 2015)*

This debate seems to give a clear indication that a range of skills is necessary to compete in the current job market. Other skills, including business, marketing, communications, fundraising, donor-relationship building, technical theatre and collaborative working are also key components for successful careers (Building a Dancer, 2018) Studies of dance talent development support this anecdotal evidence, finding that talent characteristics are multidimensional, applying motivation, commitment and coping skills to physical, technical and artistic skill development (Walker et al., 2010). The multidimensional nature of dance talent development requires an interdisciplinary approach (Redding et al., 2011). Psychological skills, such as resilience, self-regulation, creativity and grit, may be valuable assets to a dance professional within a constantly fluctuating job market. Thus far, such skills have not been an explicit part of dance talent development.

Your Role

This book is intended for parents, teachers and aspiring dancers. It is not intended to be an academic text, nor will it provide a comprehensive overview of literature or academic sources. It is written in a practical and approachable way, and one we as authors hope will make this book instructive without being prescriptive or impenetrable. It incorporates our views, which are informed by academic research, as well as practical experience working with athletes and dancers. The content of the book covers how aspiring dancers may develop their goals and, ultimately, define what success means to them. A toolbox of strategies is drawn from selected literature, including our own, to apply to talent development pathways, exemplar experiences of excellent performers and a planning section to plot actions based on evidence and trustworthy advice.

The Book's Structure

The book is divided into four parts: Ideas, Tools, Realities and Action.

Ideas

Part I focuses on how aspiring dancers, and those that support them, generate and refine their thinking about what they want to achieve. In this section, our focus is on the ability to define, reflect on and question goals using creative and flexible thinking, and to set those goals harmoniously within the larger frame of your life. The aim of this section is to

INTRODUCTION

answer this question: 'What is the dream for me?' In Chapter 1, we examine the common preparatory steps for lifelong achievement and satisfaction, whatever your goal, as well as recognizing that goals will regularly change. However, fundamental to this chapter is the recognition that there is no one way – the best approach is to use flexible and adaptable methods that are suited to your targets, and focus on being the best that you can be and enjoying it. The chapter also looks at the subjectivity of definitions of success in dance based on genre, differing goals and how defining aims in specific terms will help determine the ultimate path to success.

Tools

Part II equips dancers, and those that support them, to understand the current literature and knowledge in talent development. The aim is to build a toolbox and fill it with possible strategies to select from using critical thinking and self-reflection.

Chapter 2 introduces the Psychological Characteristics of Developing Excellence (PCDEs). Psychological skills and characteristics are key determinants of development and performance. A common characteristic of dancers who make it to the top could arguably be the possession and deployment of a range of psychological skills that enable performers to cope with the varied challenges they encounter on their journey. Alongside this, expert dancers will also likely have the confidence to 'have a go' and stay with the journey when faced with the setbacks and challenges that are an inevitable part of the process. Embedding the teaching and testing of PCDEs into dance training using formal, informal and procedural structures is an effective talent development strategy.

Chapter 3 addresses the psychomotor or physical demands of dance training. This chapter stresses that early training will encompass a broad range of skills, wider than the demands of dance, and will develop confidence to perform those skills effectively. This critically well-considered early training can counter many of the issues associated with early specialization, make for a healthier dancer and result in a better adult performer.

Chapter 4 provides a brief introduction to talent identification and development pathways in dance and discusses factors that talented individuals, parents or teachers can consider to ensure this crucial process delivers what is needed to reach the goals in mind. Traditional methods for recognizing talent, what talent may look like and why, and what to look for in talent development environments are discussed.

Part II finishes with a focus on supporting dancers' mental health, including mental health issues related to performance, as well as to life in general in Chapter 5. A combination of performer skills, perspective and knowledge, coupled with decreased stigma, can help to counter these issues and to promote positive growth. Preparation, challenge and positivity within talent development environments can develop flexibility and adaptability in developing performers. Teachers can support dancers' mental health through the application of Seligman's PERMA model (Seligman, 2018) and parents can provide support tailored to the values of their child and employ a nested approach to support, whereby their role is gradually adjusted from manager to consultant.

Realities

In Part III, we discuss common challenges that dancers, and those that support them, may experience. Through observation, self-awareness, courage and confidence, challenge and failure create opportunities for growth. Chapter 6 outlines factors that might hinder progression and impact on the young dancer, such as perfectionism, passion, fear of failure, identity foreclosure and the evaluative nature of dance education. Ultimately, the chapter emphasizes how challenge can be an important developmental tool on the young dancer's journey.

Action
Part IV closes the book with guidance on how to make decisions based on evidence and trustworthy advice. Effective, iterative goal-setting based on evidence, best practice, an informed sense of self-worth and realistic knowledge of ability are explored through the lens of thinking like a scientist. Chapter 7 explores the care necessary to ensure that there is an evidence base for choices made in the talent development environment, the need to be a critical consumer of information and to employ Sagan's Baloney Detection Kit when weighing up information and taking action.

Broader Connections

This book forms one part of a larger research project. The project aims to provide an evidence base for the value of improving dancers' psychological skill development within the talent development process to support mental health and enhance career success. By enhancing the practical evidence base, tools and information to implement evidence into practice will follow to help dancers make the most of their training and to reach their real potential, as well as empowering them to be autonomous decision-makers – or choosing the goals and leading the action to get to them.

The project will enhance practical understanding of dance talent development by investigating perceptions and observation of psychological skills development in dance talent development processes. The connection of psychological skills to career success, and mechanisms that allow skill development during dance training will follow.

The perceptions of dance students who are in training, professional dancers who have been through training and gatekeepers who select talent for training will shed light on whether psychological skills are believed to be developed during the talent development process, and the usefulness of psychological skills in determining professional success for dancers.

Perceptions of the mechanisms that may allow dancers to transform challenging experiences from talent development environments and life into successful professional experiences will also be investigated. Previous research in sport has suggested that there is a relationship between talent and trauma (Collins & MacNamara, 2012). There are indications from retrospective research that recovery from memorable challenge experiences in sportspeople depends on pre-existing adaptive psychological skills and characteristics (such as focus, motivation, self-awareness, reflection and evaluation, and self-belief), which are tested and enhanced by trauma experiences, as well as social support and an ability to apply learning from previous experiences to current challenges, e.g. post-traumatic growth (Savage et al., 2017). Further, evidence among professional performing artists indicates that, although they were more anxious and experienced more cumulative post-traumatic events in adulthood, engagement with creative experience was heightened among those with exposure to substantial childhood adversity (Thomson & Jaque, 2018). Similarly, a study examining largely early career professional dancers indicated that 34 per cent were moderately or often mentally healthy (e.g. flourishing) whilst, perhaps surprisingly, also experiencing symptoms of mental illness (Ascenso, 2018). These two states can occur at the same time within the same individual. Thus, challenge may, when combined with social support and adaptive psychological skills, lead to an ability to achieve professional success, but creative

INTRODUCTION

performers may also require support to navigate mental ill-health and trauma.

The current project is set in the understanding that dance talent development is a traditional, applied practice, and thus has limited connections to evidence or research. We also aim to enhance the relationship between practice and evidence in dance talent development by:

- Comparing amount, findings, quality, readership and impact of non-academic literature and academic literature on psychological skills in dance talent development and successful professional dance careers.
- Grounding the current programme of research in practical environments, led by the needs and outcomes required for practitioners, and adding this to the body of peer-reviewed literature.
- Engaging current stakeholders in reflection on, and development of, a practice-led and evidence-based intervention to develop psychological skills among talented young dancers.

Integrating the perceptions gathered with previous evidence from sport and dance, in the second part of the project, we will pilot a programme to see whether dance talent development pathways can achieve mental health outcomes and professional success by: (1) supporting the development of (and confidence in deploying) effective, targeted and appropriate psychological skills for performance (Collins & MacNamara, 2017); and (2) supporting young dancers to make informed, autonomous decisions about talent-enhancing activities, with balanced understanding of risks and benefits for health and performance.

SUMMARY

In summary, elite professional dance careers are physically, psychologically and economically challenging and, thus, professional success requires robust preparation of varied characteristics. Psychological skills are a defining feature of expert performance in other domains and are also anecdotally perceived to support success in professional dance careers.

However, limited evidence exists to suggest the specific psychological characteristics required for success, or the mechanisms, factors and timing that allow for their development. We are engaged in a programme of research to better understand these phenomena in practice and share this understanding with academics and practitioners.

In this book, we present a unique approach of plain-spoken suggestion and information provision on this subject as coaches, parents, scientists, advocates for dancers' health and experienced practitioners ourselves.

It is our hope that this book continues a path towards an articulated and evolving understanding of what is needed to excel in a professional career in dance, with specific emphasis on the systematic and purposeful development of psychological characteristics required for excellent performance.

PART I

IDEAS

Dancers and those that support them can use this section to generate and refine their thinking about what they want to achieve.

Skills: self-reflection, questioning, confidence, motivation, harmonious passion, creative and flexible thinking.
Outcome: To define what success will look like for you.

What is the dream?

What do you want? Each individual can use this book to help achieve the best that they are capable of and wish to commit to.

CHAPTER 1

PARAMETERIZING THE CHALLENGE: WHICH WAY IS *THE* WAY?

What Do *You* Want? (Fig. 1.1)

If you have picked up this book, you are clearly interested in dance. It is always sensible to get as much information as possible as you plan your future or try to support a family member or others towards success.

Before we start, however, it is worth considering those goals in slightly more detail, starting with what the book you are holding aims to do. This book is not about how to guarantee success in a dance career, although the advice and information included here could be used to significantly improve your preparation and, therefore, your chances of reaching that goal. This is a book about how to nurture young talented individuals by supporting their potential and intelligence, and by preparing them to realize their best possible outcome. The eventual goal could be an elite performance on stage, committed involvement in a non-performing role in the dance profession, or a career doing something meaningful and fulfilling and completely unrelated to dance. The main point is that each individual can use this book to help achieve the best that they are capable of and wish to commit to. Furthermore, each person can achieve their goals, recognizing that these may change with time and experience.

A person can aim at any time for performances that fit into one of three categories,

Figure 1.1 This figure comes from a project looking at the 'life pathways' that participants in a variety of different sports and physical activities could follow. The 'Three Worlds' Continuum (developed from Jess & Collins, 2003). Adapted from 'Participant development in sport: An academic review', Bailey et al. (2010). Sports Coach UK, 4, 1–134.

relating to their own personal goals. These are as follows:

- ERE or Elite Referenced Excellence. In ERE, your ability is measured by your status against others or through competition. For example, 'I'm a principal dancer at XXX', 'I toured with XXX', 'I won the YYY prize/competition' or 'I am the XXX world champ'.
- PRE or Personally Referenced Excellence. In PRE, your ability is based on how you have developed in relation to your own past performance. For example, 'After all that hard-focused practice, I can see my skills improving' or 'I feel I am performing and competing much better recently'.

PARAMETERIZING THE CHALLENGE: WHICH WAY IS *THE* WAY?

- PSW or Physical Self Worth. In PSW, your involvement in dance is a personally beneficial thing. 'I dance because I enjoy it, it helps me stay fit, it makes me feel good about myself, or I just love the environment and people associated with it.' This could also be 'I love it. After dance classes, I feel energized and at one with myself.' or 'Dance is important in my life. I just *am a dancer*'.

Basic Movement Competence

Finally, note that your ability to be successful in any of the categories above, or to move between them, is built on a base of sound movement skills. This will be covered in Chapter 3.

The aim is to equip you for the experience and level you want. These 'three worlds' are not distinct categories; they are a continuum. Further, one is not any 'better' than the others; it depends on what you want.

Finally, you can pick a pathway through the worlds as you progress. Some people will be driven to perform in the ERE world when they are young, then perhaps move towards PRE or even PSW as they gain more experience. Others will come later to performance, seeking an ERE/PRE combination when they are older. The point is to know where you are going, as this makes it easier to plan and focus. We will cover this in the next chapter. For the moment, keep in mind one of the mantras that will recur throughout this book: 'It depends.'

A Note About 'Eliteness'

Throughout this book, when we discuss elite excellence, we are referring to the contexts where individuals are either performing professionally or training intensively or competitively with the intended outcome of a professional career as a performer. Although we recognize that motives, levels of engagement, short- and long-term professional goals, and, importantly, potential or ability, can and will change. As such (1) not all 'elite' dancers in training or professional careers are inherently competitive or focused on engaging with dance at a constant, intensive level, (2) those participating recreationally may have competitive or intensive engagement with dance at times, (3) both groups may engage in dance out of a variety of motivations – a love for movement, a desire for a benefit that dance brings, or outside pressures and (4) that your engagement with dance may (and probably will) change throughout your life – whether you are a professional who retires or someone who dances recreationally and suddenly changes pathways into a professional career at an unexpected time.

How Might You Get There?

IDENTIFYING GOALS

Before continuing, take a moment to think about Elite Referenced Excellence, Personally Referenced Excellence, and Physical Self Worth.

Go back and read through what they mean once more, and decide which one is relevant in your situation, right now. Try to be focused on what is happening now, rather than thinking too much about the future (or the past). If it helps, consider how this goal may have changed over time, but try to come back to what it is right now.

Next, consider why this is the goal now. There is no right or wrong answer but be aware of the reason for the choice you've made.

Once you have thought about this, write down what the goal is right now and how it relates to either ERE, PRE or PSW.

PARAMETERIZING THE CHALLENGE: WHICH WAY IS *THE* WAY?

What is the goal right now and how does it relate to ERE, PRE or PSW?

Continuing the 'it depends' theme, we must emphasize that, just as there are myriad goals or motivations in dance, there is also no one way to achieve them. Rather, what we offer is a set of principles, together with a variety of tools and considerations, focused on preparing you for whatever path you wish to take or opportunities that arise. In other words, each suggestion is conditional on what you want, who you are (your particular strengths and weaknesses, plus age and stage of development) and the dance style or styles that you wish to pursue. Interestingly, our own research suggests that the types of activity and approaches suitable for those focused on top-level performance or lower-level participation are a good deal closer than many have suggested (cf. Collins & Bailey, 2015). Please don't be surprised if, after careful consideration of alternatives, your plan ends up with several features common to someone else's, even though they have a completely different set of targets. The whole thing won't be totally the same but there are several principles that apply across the three worlds' spectrum. We cover these ideas in the 'Defining Success' box, where quotes from dancers illustrate how widely things can vary but also what core similarities exist.

DEFINING SUCCESS

No book or person can definitively describe how to become a successful dancer, but tools and support exist to help fulfil potential and reach goals, no matter what they are. Although the idea of following a recipe for success sounds very tempting, for a recipe to work, the assumption would be that all success looks the same. However, success in dance isn't just one thing, and more often than not, it looks different for different people.

How do you define success? Take a minute now and imagine your future, successful self. What is that person doing?

Definitions of success could be based on others' expectations, examples of successful people you've been exposed to, on values or beliefs. It might also be based on whether skills and success are judged based on the star factor (ERE), self-development and improvement (PRE) or purely on loving the feeling of dancing (PSW). The important thing to remember is that 'it depends'.

---

continued

PARAMETERIZING THE CHALLENGE: WHICH WAY IS *THE* WAY?

To get to future successes, you need to have an idea of which way you are going. You might already know (and have started on your way), but if you're not sure yet, you can start by asking yourself some questions:

- Is dance your only passion or one of many?
- Is dance a career or purely for enjoyment?
- Do you see yourself:
    ◊ Under the spotlight or behind the scenes?
    ◊ Creating the next big creative idea or being a great interpreter of someone else's vision?
    ◊ Fitting into the existing world of dance or blazing a new trail?
- Are you more likely to dance in a tutu, trainers or tap shoes?
- Perhaps you'll be enjoying your own dancing style without a professional performing career?

If you are starting to feel a little bit confused – don't worry. You may not be sure yet what success will look like for you. It may take some time to think it through. And if you already know exactly what success looks like – your idea of success may just change as you continue to grow, change and develop.

Research among dancers has indicated that defining success based on factors within your control, such as learning, passion, enjoyment or love, will increase dancers' overall positive affect. (Quested and Duda, 2010).

Physical Self-Worth (PSW)

Professional dancers define success in lots of different ways, and it may help you to hear some of what they think.

I think success is like when you're feeling happy and settled in what you're doing and where you're going. Success for me as well is about lining up all the different parts of my life so that

22

PARAMETERIZING THE CHALLENGE: WHICH WAY IS *THE* WAY?

> everything is feeling on the same sort of track, personal life, professional life… and everything else. And success in terms of a professional sense… is just doing exactly what you love doing and what you want to do and… using your skills to the best of your ability.
> *Lottie, contemporary dancer and choreographer*

Is Lottie talking about being a star? No. Does that mean she isn't a talented or capable dancer? Absolutely not. She talks about enjoyment, happiness, and loving what she is doing. That sounds a lot like goals based on PSW. These kinds of goals can allow dancers greater enjoyment and increased creativity, through their focus on the sense of fulfilment they derive purely from taking part in doing something they love.

> What is being successful? Someone might say, 'Yeah, but you're not in a Hollywood movie'. I don't need to be in a Hollywood movie to be successful. I feel like just living and breathing I'm successful. Just doing what I'm doing. I'm happy. You have to be happy.
> *Sam, West End and commercial dancer*

Research among dancers has indicated that defining success based on factors within your control, such as learning, passion, enjoyment or love, will increase dancers' overall positive affect (Quested & Duda, 2010). Do you think success is about being happy? Although well-being is a desirable and constructive outcome, it may not be the primary outcome for those striving for transcendent performance, or those focused on the external trappings of success.

Elite Referenced Excellence (ERE)

> My most joyful time when I'm performing is opening night because you know you've worked so hard in rehearsals. Rehearsals are a killer – in the tech period, millions of notes, and then you and your body – your sore, tired body – get through to the first night's show and you're like, 'I've done this now. It's on my CV' [laughs]. No one can take that away from me. And that's success, because there are so many factors that could make you not be able to get to that point: not getting the job in the first place, your body giving out on you – but then to get a standing ovation on opening night – that is exceptional, as a feeling.
> *Andrew, West End dancer*

Andrew's idea of success is partially about being recognized by others, perhaps in a competitive audition or by an audience on opening night. This ERE helps Andrew to recognize his accomplishments and drives him through challenging rehearsals. This competitive focus can help crystallize motivation to reach a goal, but it can also tip over into a negative feeling when you aren't recognized by others for your talents.

The way you think about success is important in how you feel about your accomplishments. If you are only successful when someone else recognizes you – gives you that lead role, compliments you or focuses their attention and interest on you – what happens if no one notices you? Do you suddenly lose all your confidence? Do you feel like you aren't capable any more?

Some dancers might be very focused on whether they can make dance a career and be paid for their time, but that may not be the only thing that is important.

> Success as a dancer for me is being paid to dance… I also think there's something to be said for doing what you want to do versus doing any sort of work. To me, success is working in the field you want to be in… not just taking a job because it's a job. Yeah, I guess it's maintaining something – health – physical and mental. And that's probably a lot more long-term

PARAMETERIZING THE CHALLENGE: WHICH WAY IS *THE* WAY?

> interpretation of success for me if you're able to be okay as a dancer. Mentally and psychologically for a period – that is a definition of success.
>
> *James, contemporary dance artist*

James talks about making money, but also about how satisfying he finds the work he is doing. Where do you think that satisfaction comes from?

Personally Referenced Excellence (PRW)

Success for a dancer may also include maintaining physical and psychological health alongside a career in dance.

> Being able to – healthfully – push yourself further than you have been able to before, and to achieve something that you wanted to achieve, and you perhaps weren't sure whether you'd be able to achieve it – and you manage to achieve it. That doesn't have to be big things… I think you can book a job and be very unhappy, and I don't think that's success. I think booking a great job, being happy, having a good work–life balance, having a good social circle, doing the best you can in your job – I think that's success.
>
> *Grace, West End dancer*

Grace talks about PRE, surpassing her own abilities through hard work. But notice how her motivations have changed over time. She talks about doing certain jobs, but realizes that if they didn't make her happy, that perhaps they weren't worth the work she had to put into them. Remember that throughout your life you continue to learn, and your experiences can change what you think about success.

Trying to suggest a master plan for dance development is an impossibly complex, moving target. Consequently, please see all our suggestions as conditional; pick and choose to develop your own *optimum blend*, designed for your own targets and taste.

Of course, blending can be difficult. Therefore, a major factor in making sure your blend works optimally is knowing *why* certain ideas are suggested; plus, ideally, having an idea of *how* they work.

QUESTIONS TO CONSIDER

You may not agree with what the dancers above have said, but do you know what success is for you? What does it mean to 'make it'? What makes a dancer 'one of the best'? Do you want to be talented, celebrated or have critical acclaim? Would you like to be influential, popular, sought after, known outside of dance and within? Do you want to have a transcendent, unique performance style? Do you want to make a living from your talent?

Definitions of success are subjective but very important. They are also often multifaceted, with any one individual describing success through their own personal blend of the ideas described by this sample of performers. Whatever your personal viewpoint, however, it is worth thinking through your motivations and using significant others (including friends, family and teachers) to work out what you are after. To achieve success, you first need to know where you are going. Then you need to work out what you need to do to get there. It is also important to note that your motivations may change as you mature, gain experience or even get to see other alternatives. Progress, satisfaction and happiness can all depend on having some clear ideas on this… don't hesitate to reflect and revise as you develop.

Blending Principles – an Example of Practice

Let's imagine that you are learning a new technique or movement; one that is quite challenging, and which needs some repetition to really get it right. Your choices, in this case, are whether to really focus on that one technique or movement, perhaps neglecting other stuff, or to keep it as a part of your overall class routine. Choosing between these two extremes, what scientists call blocked or variable practice, is a classic 'it depends' scenario.

Blocked practice, doing the move or technique repeatedly, is more effective at quick development – if you need it for a show this coming weekend and it is key to your routine/performance, then get practicing/rehearsing. You might also use this approach if you are a bit nervous about making mistakes… the practicing/rehearsing (what we call *embedding*; Carson & Collins, 2015) will help to establish the skill *and* build your confidence. These are some reasons that musicians often stress the importance of long, focused hours (known as *deliberate practice*) as a core feature of their development.

Consider an alternative, however, where you are learning several moves as part of a longer-term development programme. You might be in full-time training, for example, or simply taking regular classes to build your basics. In both cases, you have time on your side, with no imminent need to be on top of this skill. In this case, mixing up your practice, so that the target move is executed in association with a variable mix of others, is the optimum approach. The variability, constantly challenging your brain to 'sort out' and execute different moves, although more difficult for you, develops adaptability and almost builds a 'stronger' or more robust-to-pressure skill.

It depends can apply to all sorts of things, including the way in which you might practice or get taught in a class situation. As we have mentioned already, neither of these two approaches is better than the other. It simply depends on what your goal is and the context in which you are working. Clarify those, then think through the advice in this book to see which practice ingredients, and in which blend, will give you the optimum outcome.

It's also worth considering how the blend might change with time, experience or other elements of context. As a rule, variable practice is the best option for the longer-term development process. As you get closer to performance, however, there is an obvious point to focusing your practice more specifically. You might use both approaches concurrently, with each employed for a particular purpose. For example, professional dancers would recognize the distinction between morning classes (keeping an eye on your general development) and afternoon rehearsals, concentrating on preparation for the evening performance.

One other thing: you do have to get off the fence here… no doing both and thinking that is an effective compromise. This is also a good example of where training harder is not the answer (more on this in later chapters). Training smarter is what we are suggesting… knowing why and what you should be doing to optimally achieve your own personal goals.

Unfortunately, some of these blending guidelines are 'either/or'… Each session is designed to optimally meet its goals. Even though the sessions take place on the same day, they are fulfilling very different purposes. We will return to this idea in

PARAMETERIZING THE CHALLENGE: WHICH WAY IS *THE* WAY?

Chapter 3. Physical preparation will often incorporate several different methods in a weekly schedule, with each focused on an end goal.

The Dancer as Critical Reflector

The best idea is always to be clear about *why* you are doing *what* you are doing and take the trouble to check whether the *why* or *how* you are doing it is the optimum solution for that need. Don't worry… this is genuinely complex, and many different opinions will exist – especially in some styles of dance where tradition is key. The main thing is that you develop and employ your skills of *critical reflection*, asking questions of yourself and others to ensure the best blend and your confidence in it.

For example, you might always have been required to do a warm-up to a very specific pattern, in terms of both length and content. However, we also know that variations in this are usual, especially as dancers mature or to meet individual needs. Reflecting on the why of what you do, whilst keeping mind, ears and eyes open to see how others approach things, can offer you some useful insights and alternatives to consider (and experiment with as the 'Critical reflections' box will show).

Interestingly, pursuing this kind of deep knowledge in their own development, how the process works and what choices are available, is a common marker across high-performance environments. Ranging across sport, music, the military, high-level business and, of course, dance, those destined for the top will take a specific interest in what is done with/to them, asking questions and increasing their knowledge base. Of course, some do this with a view to a subsequent career in teaching or coaching the activity, but even those who leave the domain will rise higher if they pursue knowledge. As an important additional point, knowing and understanding the components of your development, knowing why they are there and how things might be tweaked to meet specific challenges along the way, also helps build your confidence: both in what you are doing and how effective it will be. The knowledge also helps the performer to tweak, refine and transfer ideas, helping them cope with new challenges as they occur, or even anticipating and developing the tools to handle them before they emerge.

Knowing and understanding the components of your development, knowing why they are there and how things might be tweaked to meet specific challenges along the way, helps to build your confidence. It also helps you to cope with new challenges as they occur, or to anticipate and develop the tools to handle them before they emerge.

PARAMETERIZING THE CHALLENGE: WHICH WAY IS *THE* WAY?

The Dancer as Scientist

Another feature of the deep knowledge described above is the degree to which any performer knows what works for them personally, why that is and alternative ways in which these needs can be met. This idea is always helped by the performer doing some experimentation, literally developing and trying out some variations to see what generates the best results. This was certainly seen as a key feature of critical reflection by Schön (1983), whose work underpins much of the critical reflection approach. We have developed these ideas as a feature of our own work with performance psychologists (e.g. Martindale & Collins, 2005) and coaches (e.g. Abraham & Collins, 2011) on how they experiment, either practically or in mental simulation, to try out ideas in advance of applying them. Referred to as Professional Judgement and Decision-Making (PJDM), this would certainly be a useful feature for dance teachers and those concerned with the management and promotion of performance, such as artistic directors. Furthermore, as explored in Chapter 2, developing a degree of self-awareness, as well as personal skills of self-regulation, are important tools to facilitate your development along the pathway.

For a variety of reasons, doing some self-experimentation, both to find out what works best for you as a performer and to

Self-experimentation, both to find out what works best for you as a performer and to build your confidence in these approaches, is a positive approach to determine what works for you, why that is and alternative ways in which these needs can be met.

PARAMETERIZING THE CHALLENGE: WHICH WAY IS *THE* WAY?

- All our advice is conditional – it will vary based on individual characteristics, dance style, and your goals. Remember that *it depends*.
- It is important to think about what success means to you, and what kinds of goals you hope to achieve. Defining where you aim to get to in specific terms will help you to determine your path. And, remember, defining success is subjective. No two people are likely to think success is the same.
- There is no *one* way – methods must be flexible and adaptable, optimized towards your own targets.
- Deep knowledge of what your aims are, how you might best pursue them, plus why and why not certain approaches are preferable is always useful.
- Be the best you can be.
- Do what you can do and love it.

The style(s) of dance you experience may have very different subjective outlooks on what success for dancers should or could be. Get to know which styles challenge and inspire you the most. Likely this means you'll want to try a few.

PARAMETERIZING THE CHALLENGE: WHICH WAY IS *THE* WAY?

Chapter 1: Commentary

This chapter contextualizes the parameters of a developing career in dance, and possibly beyond, by exploring three important clear categories. Personally, as an educator of dance teachers and dancers, I view this as incredibly pertinent in managing the goals and expectations of dancers with a balance between their physical and emotional development. It is useful in developing, our own and of the dancers that we are training, an increased awareness of specific psychological states and how these directly affect how we then measure success against set goals. This idea is further supported by an explanation that these goals most likely will change and, therefore, having an increased awareness of these fluctuations enables the viewing of these changes in a more positive light, rather than with critical and potentially harmful judgement.

I often hear how dance teachers are dismayed that a student's goals have changed or, from the dance teachers' perspective, have decreased, i.e. that they 'no longer wish to audition for...' or that they 'do not want to attend the additional classes for examinations', essentially bemoaning the fact that the student is no longer invested in physical goals. These statements do not acknowledge that it is OK for that student to change their goals, rather than the focus being the fulfilment of the goals of the teacher.

Many dance teachers and vocational training providers measure the success of their students only by the grade they achieve or by the dance job they win. In contrast this chapter explains that defining success is incredibly subjective and most probably transitory, moving the focus back to the student's or dancer's ability to measure their own success. This is supported by an insightful explanation of the process and the fact that it can be daunting. This enables confidence that it is fine not to have all the answers all the time. As a dance educator this knowledge is imperative as we take responsibility in the studio of realizing each and every student's potential, and the fact that each student does not aspire to be a star is vital to our pedagogic approach.

The inclusion of examples of blending principles is critical to our planning and to training our students smarter. Many teachers complain that they are frustrated with the lack of progress on 'cleaning' a dance, and so on, without awareness that the issue is not with the dancers but with the planning and delivery of rehearsals and classes. If these strategies were embedded in a more focused way into a young dancer's training, they would then be able to make use of these for themselves proficiently as professionals. Additionally, the development of critical reflection as a method of enhancing knowledge and understanding is a vital tool that is still missing from most classes/rehearsals. The main form of feedback often still comes from the teacher and the value of peer or self-evaluation as an effective learning strategy is not utilized. In this chapter I am greatly encouraged that this reflective process is being outlined as having a key role. In a recent lecture that I gave for developing dance teachers, the pertinent message of the day was to make use of a reflective models, i.e. Schön (1983), not only to critically evaluate your own pedagogic practice, but to additionally facilitate the process in students.

The focus of the success of dancers is that the need to be aware of their own process, both physically and emotionally, is incredibly valuable. This student-centred approach, as initially outlined by theorists early on in the twentieth century, including John Dewey, Jean Piaget and Lev Vygotsky, is now long overdue in the world of dance training. It is exciting to see the value of this explained and contextualized with the professional world of dance today, and may it enhance the development of current and future dancers.

Sam Le Bihan (BA Hons, PGCE, RT bbodance) has been Head of Teaching Qualifications at bbodance since 2015. At appointment she was responsible for writing a new programme of study that reflected current practice for dance teachers that has resulted in an innovative and highly successful teaching training programme.

The programme supports the value of traditional dance training, whilst being informed by current good practice, with the focus on the physical, social and emotional development of dancers. In September 2018, Sam successfully completed the writing and development of a bbodance Level 1 Contemporary Dance syllabus, fully Ofqual recognized, and Level 2 will be completed in 2020. Additionally, Sam maintains a private teaching practice and delivers a range of classes and workshops for dance students and professional dance teachers.

PART 2

TOOLS

Dancers and those that support them can use this section to understand the current literature and knowledge in talent development.

Skills: critical thinking, self-reflection.
Outcome: building a toolbox and filling it with possible strategies.

What tools and strategies will support you to reach your goals?

The possession of psychological skills is crucial for both development and performance. Even if a dancer has lots of natural ability, converting potential into excellence is contingent on the deployment of a range of skills, such as commitment, motivation and determination, which allows young dancers to interact effectively with the developmental opportunities encountered during training.

CHAPTER 2

INTRODUCTION TO PSYCHOLOGICAL CHARACTERISTICS OF DEVELOPING EXCELLENCE

There is a considerable evidence base for the role of psychological characteristics as determinants of both development (MacNamara et al. 2010a, b; Rees et al., 2013) and performance (Orlick & Partington, 1988; Sloboda, 2000; Issurin, 2017). A simple way of thinking about this is to consider what mindset a dancer needs to achieve their potential and to perform at the highest level. Of course, if mindset is important, and few would agree that it isn't, consider how it is generated so that young dancers can develop the psychological skills and adaptability required to negotiate the inevitable challenges of development (Rees et al., 2016).

In this chapter, we will start to unpick the mental skills, behaviours and characteristics that young dancers need in order to optimize development opportunities (e.g. performance opportunities), adapt to setbacks (e.g. injury, slumps in performance) and effectively negotiate key transitions (e.g. moving into the professional dance world) encountered along the pathway to excellence. The possession of these psychological skills is crucial; even if a dancer has lots of natural ability, converting potential into excellence is contingent on the deployment of a range of skills, such as commitment, motivation and determination, that allows young dancers to interact effectively with the developmental opportunities encountered during training.

Of course, equipping young dancers with psychological skills will not necessarily result in high-level performance, since there is a wide range of variables that influence the likelihood of reaching the top (see Chapter 4). However, it will provide aspiring young dancers with the capacity and competencies to strive to reach their potential. Indeed, you can probably name some dancers who were not stand-out performers during their early years, or who didn't seem to have the ideal physical or technical profile to be successful, but were able to compensate for some perceived weaknesses through increased effort, determination and commitment to the learning process. Likewise, you are probably familiar with dancers who were identified as the next big star during their early years but who failed to reach their potential and either dropped out completely, or performed at lower levels than would be expected because they did not possess, or appropriately deploy, the psychological skills necessary to maximize developmental opportunities and to cope with the challenges they encountered. It seems that psychological skills, and the ability to deploy them appropriately, might be the difference between who makes and who doesn't.

The Nature versus Nurture Debate

A common question in talent development is the extent to which the individual's skill is a product of innate ability *or* learning and experience. Indeed, understanding the balance of genetic inheritance and environmental factors that might contribute to the manifestation of talent has an important role in how young dancers are taught and developed. Even though there is anecdotal evidence of 'untrained talent' emerging in some domains, this is unlikely to occur in such technical pursuits as the various forms of dance. Likewise, even though some physical and physiological variables are clearly advantageous in some disciplines of dance, there is little evidence for 'hardware' advantages between the professional or competitive elite or those participating with a more recreational focus. For these reasons, the nature stance – attributing the differences in those who make it and those who do not to the presence or absence of physical attributes – does not have much support. Instead, it is important to focus on the interaction of genetic factors, psychological factors and a favourable practice environment, rather than based on one of these factors in isolation (Abbott et al., 2005; Gagné, 2008).

What clearly results from this discussion is the need to distinguish between determinants of *performance* and determinants of *development*. Unfortunately, when working with young performers, emphasis is on determinants of performance: what makes a performer good right now, rather than fostering what helps them get good in the longer term. This is an important distinction as there is little causative evidence to suggest that the best high-level performers show, or must show, significant signs of promise during their early involvement. Indeed, many world-class performers were not identified as talented during their formative years but still managed to succeed (Abbott & Collins, 2004). Therefore, if exceptional performances at a young age are 'neither a necessary nor a sufficient prerequisite for later success' (Vaeyens et al., 2009, p.1370), why do they form the basis of how young dancers are selected and developed early in their careers? Focusing on the factors that both encourage young performers to engage in, and then persist at, dance training would seem the more useful starting point in terms of talent development.

Talent as a Developmental Construct

A key message throughout this book is that talent should be viewed as developmental and multidimensional. This suggests that certain behaviours only emerge when the supporting subsystems and processes are ready. This understanding of talent has important repercussions for how teachers work with young dancers at the start of the pathway.

First, it points to the importance of considering, identifying and developing *all* the factors that, over the course of time, may promote development. A young dancer might be selected into a conservatoire because of their 'obvious' dance ability but once in that environment their development and progress stalls. For example, they might lack the commitment required to invest the requisite hours of training or the self-regulation necessary to engage in independent practice. Equally, luck (Bailey, 2007) and individual factors, such as injury, illness, specific learning difference and medical issues, may not only affect performance indicators, such

PSYCHOLOGICAL CHARACTERISTICS OF DEVELOPING EXCELLENCE

An individual with a growth mindset views ability as developmental and reflective of the effort they exert on the task. Challenge is viewed as an exciting part of learning and, rather than fearing failure, failure is seen as a necessary part of the learning journey.

as attendance, marks and progression, but also require significant coping skills from the dance student. A clued-in teacher or parent will recognize this and spend time working with the dancer to develop the psychological skills required. As a result of this intervention, the development and deployment of characteristics such as motivation, determination and confidence can result in unexpected and sudden changes in development and performance, reflecting a multiplicative conception of talent (Simonton, 1999).

A young dancer may have excellent physical characteristics, but they may also require outstanding musical ability, a sense of rhythm, artistic abilities, stage presence and the psychological skills to engage in the development process in order to be successful. In fact, psycho-behavioural skills may act as catalysts of development enabling young dancers to maximize their potential and make the most of the teaching and learning opportunities available to them. The 'multiplicative' understanding of talent means that if any of these

PSYCHOLOGICAL CHARACTERISTICS OF DEVELOPING EXCELLENCE

components of talent is missing, then all the other factors will lose their value. As such, it seems reasonable to focus on teasing out and deliberately promoting the individual skills and characteristics required to meet developmental challenges and transitions to support young dancers.

The Psychological Skills Required for Development (Fig. 2.1)

Attitude

There is a consensus that having the 'right attitude' to succeed is an essential component of successful development in any domain. Carol Dweck (2006), for example, proposes that there are two types of mindsets: a fixed mindset and a growth mindset. An individual with a fixed mindset views ability as permanent and judges situations in terms of how they reflect upon their ability: if I have a bad performance, I am a bad dancer. This type of mindset has important implications for talent development: individuals with a fixed mindset will rarely seek out opportunities to learn or be challenged because failure would be reflective of their ability. Instead, they choose activities that are 'safe' and where achievement is easily attainable; performers with a fixed mindset fear failure and withhold effort as a means of self-protection against this failure. In a competitive world where dancers need to adapt to a range of roles and challenges, a fixed mindset can be the stumbling block to progress.

In contrast, an individual with a growth mindset views ability as developmental and reflective of the effort they exert on the task. Challenge is viewed as an exciting part of learning and rather than fearing failure, failure is seen as a necessary part of the learning journey. An individual with a growth mindset views a poor performance as an opportunity to learn and that subsequent performance is contingent on exerting more effort: 'If I try harder, I will get better'.

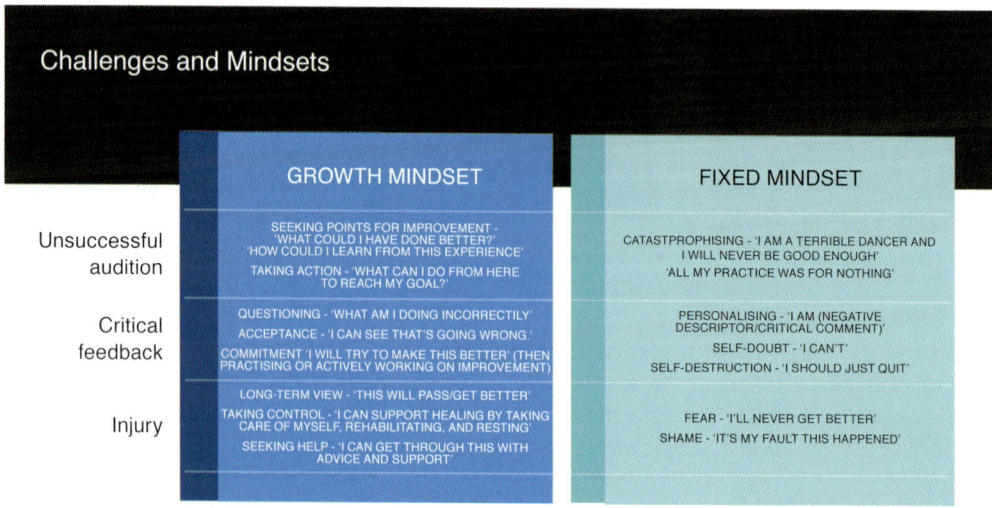

Figure 2.1 Examples of growth and fixed mindsets in dance.

Dweck (2006) describes the difference between a fixed and a growth mindset as 'a belief that your qualities are carved in stone (fixed mindset) leads to a host of thoughts and actions, and a belief that your qualities can be cultivated (growth mindset) leads to a host of different thoughts and actions, taking you down an entirely different road'. A young performer with a fixed mindset will not exert effort because they believe that if they were talented, they would not need to try, and that effort is a bad thing because it is reflective of inability. For young performers with a growth mindset, effort is the lynchpin that allows them to realize their potential, practice leads to success. A growth mindset allows young performers to understand that their talents and abilities can be developed through effort and persistence. The key point here is that mindset, or the attitude that young people bring to achievement domains, has a large impact on our understanding of success and failure, and subsequent engagement in developmental activities. We will return to these ideas later in this chapter.

Research has repeatedly shown that a growth mindset fosters positive attitudes toward practice and learning, leads to a hunger for feedback and a greater ability to deal with setbacks (Dweck, 2006). Self-regulation plays an important role here. Given the demands of high-level participation in dance, a self-regulated dancer who possesses a growth mindset has the ability to initiate and persist at tasks that are not inherently motivating or interesting, though nonetheless important for development. As such, an appropriate attitude to practice might be the key to optimizing the experience. This might be even more significant as the dancer progresses, and the demands and intensity of training increase. The ability to cope effectively with the stressors of development and to adapt to the challenges faced, specifically increases autonomy and responsibility for one's development as the dancer moves from education into a professional domain; they are key components of successful development. Fostering this attitude early, at home and in dance, is an essential starting point on the development journey.

As we introduced earlier in this chapter, viewing talent as a gift, something that someone innately has or does not have, is problematic for several reasons. First, it suggests that talent is a fixed capacity that can be identified early and remains stable over time. If this is the case, the role of dance education and, indeed, teachers must surely be questioned. Second, the belief that abilities are innate will have a significant impact on how individuals interact with teaching and learning opportunities. Individuals who view abilities as having innate origins often attribute someone else's performance, good or bad, to their innate level of ability. Conversely, those that believe abilities are 'developable' attribute performance to their level of effort (Dweck, 2006). Performers who believe abilities are innate and ultimately unchangeable – a fixed mindset – are more likely to react to failure and negative feedback with decreased effort and persistence, and increased negative emotions.

This leads to maladaptive behaviours on the part of the performer: an increased risk of cultivating learned helplessness, a form of self-handicapping behaviour or forms of complacency wherein individuals believe their natural talent will lead to success and subsequently decrease their effort and motivation to improve. These responses are not conducive to learning and performance, and as a result, can compromise how well the dancer does. A warning – be careful about the label you give young people as it can have significant implications on their attitude to learning.

PSYCHOLOGICAL CHARACTERISTICS OF DEVELOPING EXCELLENCE

There may also be a dark side to growth mindset: those who believe talent to be predominantly developable are more likely to respond to poor performances with increased effort and persistence. While generally viewed as a positive characteristic, over-persistence may also be a maladaptive response and itself a form of helpless behaviour (Dweck, 2006). In short, believing that talent can be developed with enough effort or practice may not be healthy or realistic. We return to these potentially maladaptive features of development in Chapter 6.

Instilling a Positive Attitude

Dweck (2006) suggested that growth mindsets can be induced with messages from the environment that talent can be developed over time with effort. This has important implications for teachers and parents. What you say, the feedback you give and how you praise success and failure, all influence young performers' attitudes, the effort they exert and how they react to success and failure. The rest of this chapter will outline some guidelines on how teachers, parents and other stakeholders can foster appropriate attitudes to development.

Developing Appropriate Mindsets

There is a danger that some approaches to teaching and training have a detrimental effect on cultivating the appropriate attitude for learning and development (Dweck, 2006). Therefore, teachers, parents and other important figures of authority should carefully consider how they praise and reward young dancers, especially with a long-term agenda in mind. As parents and teachers of young dancers, it may be that our enthusiasm for praising children for their ability, even at very young ages, instils a fixed mindset that has significant repercussions further down the line. Instead, praising the process, the young performer's effort and the strategies employed is a more effective method. Praising effort gives the young person a variable they can control – 'if I try harder, I will get better' and a means of responding to challenge, failure and mistakes. Indeed, Dweck found that praising children for their intelligence ('You must be smart at this') as opposed to their effort ('You must have worked really hard') had a massively detrimental effect on performance. Over a series of tests, children praised for effort tried harder, worked at a task longer and enjoyed challenges more than those praised for intelligence. In the same study, those praised for effort improved their test scores by 30 per cent, while those praised for intelligence saw their scores decline by 20 per cent (Dweck, 2006). If you can get your performer (or son or daughter) to share this focus in their self-evaluations, even better.

As suggested earlier in the chapter, promoting concepts that are within the control of the young dancer, such as hard work, effort and practice, seems to be the way to promote a growth mindset. It seems that young people learn better and achieve more if they believe that they hold the key, rather than it being down to how intelligent/quick/good they are or perceive themselves to be. This is especially important when you consider the length of the journey and the inevitable 'ups and downs' young dancers will experience along the way. For a young dancer at the beginning of their journey, goals can seem far away and, at times, untenable. The same can be said when a young dancer faces injury or rejection; the delayed gratification required to stay with the process, especially in times of adversity, is often a defining feature of those who make it. Teachers, parents and even peers need to encourage the young dancer to understand that development takes time and success rarely comes right away or without overcoming challenge.

Psychological Characteristics of Developing Excellence (Fig. 2.2)

The very best dancers in the world all bring something unique to their performances. In fact, the possession and deployment of psychological skills has been shown to be a causative factor of success in sport and has received considerable support, particularly in the area of self-regulation (Toering et al., 2009). If psychological skills play such an important role in development, it is important not to leave their development to chance. Reflecting on this, in this section, we present an essential set of skills, Psychological Characteristics of Developing Excellence (PCDEs), and propose that these act as the determinants of both development and performance. PCDEs encompass both the trait characteristics (the tendency to…) and the state-deployed skills (the ability to… when…) that have been shown to play a crucial role in the realization of potential in sporting (MacNamara et al., 2010a, b) and other performance environments (Pecen et al., 2016). PCDEs are not just mental skills, such as imagery or goal-setting, but also include attitudes, emotions and desires, such as commitment, using social support and self-regulation, which are essential for negotiating the talent development process. Reflecting on the importance of instilling an appropriate attitude for development, we suggest that possession and deployment of PCDEs will generate and enable the attitude needed for development. In short, teaching the psychological skills (both formally and informally) and building on experiences, whether planned or naturally occurring, will generate the attitude and growth mindset needed to make the most of your potential.

- EFFECTIVE IMAGERY
- COMMITMENT
- REALISTIC PERFORMANCE EVALUATION
- COPING WITH PRESSURE
- GOAL SETTING
- ACTIVELY SEEKING SOCIAL SUPPORT
- FOCUS AND DISTRACTION CONTROL
- SELF-AWARENESS
- PLANNING AND SELF-ORGANIZATION
- QUALITY PRACTICE

PSYCHOLOGICAL CHARACTERISTICS OF DEVELOPING EXCELLENCE

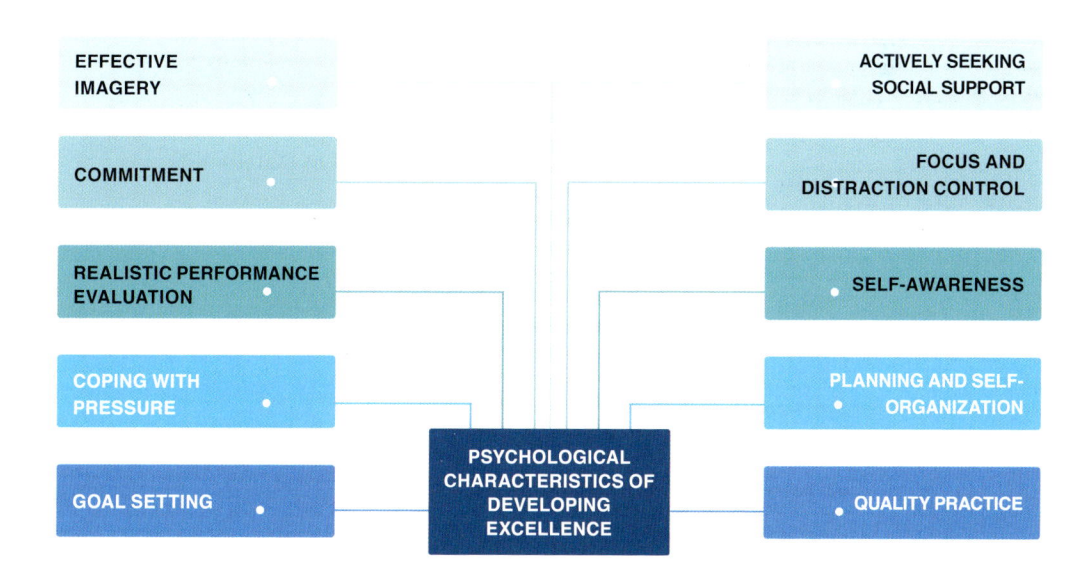

Figure 2.2 The ten behaviours consistently identified as the psychological characteristics of developing excellence (PCDEs).

PSYCHOLOGICAL CHARACTERISTICS OF DEVELOPING EXCELLENCE

PCDES IN THE CONTEXT OF DANCE

How might mental skills, attitudes, emotions and desires support dancers to make the most of their training and potentially experience successful development? Below are some examples of how PCDEs might look in dance talent development processes.

Commitment

Although Sam was understandably disappointed after not achieving her best performance in an audition, she decides to return to the next class focused on how she can improve on her musicality, which let her down in the audition.

Reuben is always looking for a chance to train with the more skilled and experienced dancers, whether in class or through the summer performance. He's always watching them and practising the skills he sees but hasn't mastered yet.

Everyone thought Charlotte's sprained ankle was going to keep her from maintaining her technique, but Charlotte found a way around not dancing by carefully planning a schedule of cross-training, seeing a physio and keeping up her memory of the choreography through an imagery programme she learned with help from the school counsellor.

Focus and Distraction Control

Just before the performance, Josh puts on his headphones and listens to his favourite playlist to relax and get into the right headspace.

After Anna recovered from her back injury, she talked about how important it was to make the most of every class and how helpful her physio had been in teaching her ways to train and rest that would help keep her body fit and healthy.

Realistic Performance Evaluation

Jess knows she is not as strong as the others in her class when it comes to fast movement, but she also knows that she is the only one in class who can remember all the choreography after seeing it just once. She is working on building up her ability to move more quickly by practising movements with a faster beat outside class and, although she knows it will take time, she's focused on training on this at least twice a week after class.

Self-Awareness

Jake was devastated when he wasn't asked to continue in the training programme he was in last year. He'd spent hours each week in the classes with the other students, and all he'd ever wanted was to train with that school. When he got home, he told his dad he wanted to have a break from dancing for a while because dancing made him feel upset. Jake made some new friends around the neighbourhood that he could play different sports with after school. Jake said he liked just having a mess around and trying out different skills. After a year, Jake started dancing again, but this time he decided to try a youth company that met once a week and made performances. Jake told his dad it was more fun dancing now that he could try out different movements, and sometimes the performances even featured some of Jake's choreography.

Coping with Pressure
Last year, Jana was selected to be the lead in the final performance. She felt that other students started behaving differently towards her, and some of them seemed to be more competitive with her in class, trying to outperform her. Janna started to feèl left out when her friends didn't invite her to after-school events any more, and she was frustrated by how critical they were of her in rehearsals. After talking with a close friend from home about how she was feeling, she decided to try to keep her head down until the performance and started going to classes outside the school and found that she met some new people.

Planning and Self-Organization
Zac always makes up his lunch on Friday night ready for his Saturday dance training. He has two dance classes in the morning and an afternoon of rehearsals, so he makes sure to have his breakfast and takes his favourite lunch and a snack. A dietician visited his dance school earlier in the year and Zac asked for help to choose some healthy foods he could bring with him to keep up his energy during his long training day.

Goal-Setting
Abby once had a teacher who asked her to write down notes, corrections and ideas after dance class, and to review the notes at the end of each week and circle things she wanted to work on especially for the following week. Abby kept up her 'Dance journal' long after she left that teacher's class, and she starts off each week with a plan for what she'll be working on.

Quality Practice
Although Ty sometimes had trouble focusing at school, he always made sure he did all the movements at dance training as well as he could – he really put in 100 per cent effort, and he liked the feeling of being properly worn out from a good training session.

Effective Imagery
Will is working on smoothing out his movement in a routine, and he's been trying to make movements connect with one another. He likes 'telling stories' with his movements, so in his head he's set out a group of words that match with how he thinks the movements should look.

Actively Seeking Social Support
When Jackie first arrived at full-time training away from home, she felt homesick all the time, found it hard to make friends with a whole new group and felt like she needed to prove her skills to her new teachers. She called home or her friends almost every night for the first month. She also started meeting one of the other new students, Ellie, for lunch each day. Ellie and Jackie talked a lot about the new teachers and traded tips on what they were learning in class. They also laughed a lot, and soon a few other students joined their lunch group, too.

PSYCHOLOGICAL CHARACTERISTICS OF DEVELOPING EXCELLENCE

PCDEs appear to be the mechanisms for achieving success and dealing with the inevitable challenges of development. If so, systematically developing these as part of a teaching approach seems sensible, especially for young dancers who show lots of promise.

PCDEs as the 'Hand of Cards' of Development

As you read this section, think of some dancers you have encountered who showed lots of promise but never quite managed to convert that potential: the young performer who couldn't perform or thrive against the pressures inherent in meeting their goals. Let's look at a couple of case studies and consider how PCDEs help young dancers to cope with the development pathway and make the most of their potential.

Early Promise Collapses Under Pressure

Although the 'next big thing' and the young dancer who shows early signs of promise are often celebrated, it is important to contextualize this against long-term goals. Ironically, an overly smooth and successful early experience may be the worst preparation for long-term success. If a young dancer hasn't had to cope with any setbacks or deal with disappointments during their early years, it is unlikely that they have developed the skills, work ethic or commitment to cope with the ebb and flow of development, especially when they enter more specialized training or performance environments. If things have been too 'easy', or they have been able to rely on exceptional physical or technical ability, then the performer might be unprepared when faced with challenges and setbacks. PCDEs appear to be the mechanisms for achieving success and dealing with the inevitable challenges of development. If so, systematically developing these as part of a teaching approach seems sensible, especially for young dancers who show lots of promise.

PSYCHOLOGICAL CHARACTERISTICS OF DEVELOPING EXCELLENCE

Dancers Have the Ability but Are Extremely Delicate

Self-regulation seems to be a distinguishing factor in who succeeds and who doesn't. Self-regulated learners have the skills to self-monitor their progress, manage their emotions, focus on self-improvement, and seek help and support from others when necessary. Conversely, young dancers without these skills do not take personal responsibility for their own development but, instead, rely on others and attribute failures to maladaptive reasons that they cannot control. Unfortunately, developing self-regulated learners is rarely a feature of development, despite the support for its benefits.

If the young performer seeks a professional career, it is worth remembering that this role comes with a great deal of individual responsibility and challenge. Providing early opportunities to develop and refine PCDEs that help performers overcome developmental challenges and stressing the process of learning how to cope independently should be key aspects of dance education.

Teach–Test–Tweak–Repeat (Fig. 2.3)

In order to ensure that the training of young dancers provides them with opportunities to develop PCDEs, we propose a 'teaching, challenging, evaluating and refining' cycle, what we will term teach–test–tweak–repeat.

Figure 2.3 Teach-test-tweak-repeat cycle of PCDE development. Adapted from 'Putting the Bumps in the Rocky Road: Optimizing the Pathway to Excellence', by Collins et al. (2016) Front. Psychol., 7:1482. doi: 10.3389/fpsyg.2016.01482.

PSYCHOLOGICAL CHARACTERISTICS OF DEVELOPING EXCELLENCE

In the 'teach' phase of this cycle, young dancers experience a gradual development of psychological skills as 'part and parcel' of their dance training, which are then tested against realistic challenges from within their environment during the 'challenge' phase. For example, a young dancer may be asked to perform with older performers, in front of a panel of teachers, or to work with a very technical piece of choreography. After the challenge, teachers and others (such as parents) engage the dancer in review – the 'tweak' phase; this process develops the dancers' capacity to evaluate and self-manage in tandem with structured feedback from teachers. As the performer progresses, both the complexity of challenge (and, therefore, the skills required) and the balance of challenge to support increases. Of course, young dancers must be given time to reflect on this process and refine the required skills. As such, enough time must be given to the dancer to learn from, develop and refine and, crucially, secure confidence in their capacity to use the skills. For example, and in order to test progress, it is also important that the young dancer can return from the challenging experience to familiar and more comfortable surroundings. This return can provide development opportunities where the dancer can freely express their newfound experiences and confidence. Indeed, this period of adaptation is essential to maximize opportunity for growth.

Crucially, the PCDE approach is most effective when it is central to, and embedded within, teaching rather than an extra part of the process. In fact, good teachers, and parents, already develop PCDEs as part of how they teach and interact with young people. The guidelines offered here build on this and propose a systematic way of including PCDEs into teaching, ensuring that they are developed purposefully and appropriately at different stages. Given the idiosyncratic nature of development, work must be individualized as much as possible, to help the dancer to explore, discover and build confidence in the blend that works best for them in their environment. This, in turn, raises the need for regular and ongoing refinement or even revision as people grow and situations change.

PCDEs in Practice

In this section, we provide some guidelines about how you might incorporate PCDEs as part of your developmental agenda. As you read, start to consider how this might play out in your environment, identifying both challenges and opportunities that must be accounted for.

Young dancers progress through various stages of training, including some who may graduate into specialized environments and then the professional world. The aim, therefore, should be that the young dancer has experienced input and application for all the PCDEs by the time they reach the end of their training. For many dancers, the transition into the professional dance world will come with varying challenges and opportunities; indeed, the various dance worlds that exist necessitate a broad blend of skills. For example, lots of auditions and classes outside of usual training might feel challenging and test self-esteem for new graduates. This developmental curriculum prepares the young dancer for the pressures they will face, such as auditions, injury, training setbacks, artistic development, and (crucially) having to make a living.

Accompanying Principles

Several other principles should be considered. First, the approach is skills-based, using a careful periodization of challenge and support to teach–test–tweak the skills, then repeat in a positive spiral. Second, the skills are taught through a combination of formal, informal and procedural methods and then tested against realistic challenges. In best practice, PCDEs are integrated as part of teaching; dancers will have to deploy PCDEs in response to challenges in their environment and the teacher can then refine and reinforce the application of the skill through feedback. After each 'teachable moment', teachers and others engage the dancer in review – what happened and why – developing their own capacity to evaluate and self-manage in tandem with structured feedback. Given the need for reflection and refinement, and recognizing that this will differ depending on the age and maturity level of the dancer, sufficient time must be given to dancers to learn from, develop and refine and, crucially, secure confidence in their capacity to use the skills.

Third, the formal part of development will usefully involve (if available) psychologist and teacher (at the least) in presenting the skill. Of course, the need for an individualized and gradual approach to the development and deployment of PCDEs is another important feature of this approach. This is backed up by a variety of informal interactions, with a teacher, psychologist, parent, other support specialist and even fellow dancers modelling effective application of the skill to realistic challenges. The procedural part also helps to keep the skills at the forefront of the process and embed them within the culture of life for the young dancer.

Fourth, the skills are taught, deployed and culturally encouraged as part of everyday practice. This does not mean that the young performers are not encouraged to deploy the skills into other areas of their life. Indeed, this is a consistent result of PCDE interventions: individuals gain confidence in their mental expertise in the studio and use this to exploit other opportunities and challenges, such as education, networking, career management and public relations/media initiatives. We do feel, however, that presenting the skills against the environment they are to be used in helps to maximize transfer. In simple terms, dancers see the skills as part of their dance development, rather than a peripheral extra bit that might be useful at some stage.

The Importance of Self-Regulation

The Irish poet Samuel Beckett's words 'Ever tried. Ever failed. No matter. Try Again. Fail again. Fail better' (1983, p.7) have a lot of resonance for how to design development opportunities for young dancers and how to debrief them as a key feature of the learning journey. Examining the biographies of some of the most successful performers, failure and setbacks are common features. In order to encourage a growth mindset and gritty (Duckworth & Duckworth, 2016) developers – the type of attitudes and behaviours that typify effective development – dance education must allow young performers to be comfortable making mistakes. In this way mistakes are seen are indicators of areas for growth and as an opportunity to learn, grow and succeed. Unfortunately, as with many other performance domains, this is not always a feature of dance education. We return to this idea later in the book, but we will now consider how your environment supports young people to develop the independence, autonomy and self-regulation needed to achieve at the highest level.

Self-regulation involves processes that enable individuals to control their thoughts, feelings, and actions and is described by Zimmerman (2000) as the extent to which individuals are metacognitively, motivationally and behaviourally proactive participants in their own learning process. Self-regulatory skills develop as early as two years of age and by the age of twelve, young people use these skills consciously in their performance environment. As such, the development of self-regulatory skills would seem a sensible focus, since these are the skills that help maximize learning and help young people balance the various demands of the pathway.

During early exposure to dance, teachers (and parents) play a major role in regulating learning – they are the ones who set goals, manage the learning environment, support and praise the young dancer, and so on. However, as performers advance, teachers should reduce that support and expect performers to take ownership of their learning and development; the young performer should take responsibility to self-regulate their learning and decide where, when, how, why and what to do. Unfortunately, this isn't always the case. Teachers, and parents, often try to do too much to support the young performer hoping to accelerate progress. Although this approach might give some short-term success, it is unlikely that the aspiring dancer is developing the self-regulatory skills that they will need when the going gets tough.

How to Do It

Self-regulation does not occur naturally but as a result of quality teaching where feedback and goal-setting are used as prompts to develop these skills. There are a couple of important things to think about here. First, the development of self-regulation skills takes time and should be purposefully embedded in dance education from the early years. Foundational skills for self-regulation are developed in the first five years of life, which means parents and teachers play an important role in helping young children regulate thinking and behaviour. Good parenting, for example, is associated with the development of self-regulation skills. A particularly good predictor is support for autonomy; letting your toddler complete a task as independently as possible, for example, by providing suggestions only when the child is stuck, seems to be a good basis for later self-regulation. As children increase their ability to act independently, teachers should turn over more of the regulating responsibilities to the children's control, while monitoring their progress and intervening when necessary to provide appropriate support. Though this can be frustrating at the time (for the parent and teacher more than the child), the long-term benefits would seem to be worth it.

How to Teach It (Fig. 2.4)

As described earlier with PCDEs, good teachers teach and reinforce self-regulation as part of their everyday interactions by modelling and scaffolding it during ordinary activities. By demonstrating and modelling appropriate behaviour, teachers (and parents and peers) show young performers how to accomplish a task and use the self-regulation needed to complete it – essentially the teaching involves bridging the gap between what the dancer already knows and can do, and the more complex skills and knowledge that they want to attain. Doing this as part of everyday experiences and interaction strengthens children's self-regulation. The process is even more powerful if parents and teachers are on the same page and there is a coherence and continuity in focus, direction and reinforcement. Of course, it is essential that no matter how exceptional the young dancer is, that developmentally appropriate expectations for children's behaviour are upheld. Even if young dancers sometimes look like adults and can perform outstandingly, they do not have cognitive and developmental maturity and, therefore, need to be treated appropriately. As such, effective teaching occurs in what is called the zone of proximal development (ZPD), which can be viewed as the 'growing edge of competence'; this represents those skills a child is ready to learn from a 'more knowledgeable other', such as a parent, peer, teacher or coach,

ACQUIRED SKILLS
What the dancer can do independently

ZONE OF PROXIMAL DEVELOPMENT
What the dancer can do with help from a more knowledgeable other (MKO)

OUT OF REACH
What the dancer cannot do yet, even with help

Figure 2.4 Vygotsky's zone of proximal development. Adapted from 'The zone of proximal development in Vygotsky's analysis of learning and instruction', Chaiklin, S. (2003). Vygotsky's educational theory in cultural context, 1, 39–64.

with scaffolding or the targeted supportive guidance that gradually reduces as the child gains skill (Vygotsky, 1930–34/1978; Copple & Bredekamp, 2009). Specifically, 'what the child is able to do in collaboration today he will be able to do independently tomorrow' (Vygotsky, 1934/1987, p.211). Therefore, be cognisant of this and recognize that expecting children to demonstrate skills outside the ZPD is ineffective and often detrimental, especially in the longterm.

In Conclusion

Developing PCDEs, and other 'above the neck' determinants of development, should enable young dancers to overcome the various roadblocks and derailers they encounter on the development pathway and allow them to make the most of their potential. This approach to development should facilitate the effective pursuit of excellence at the individual's chosen level of achievement, and serendipitously but very positively, achievement in other domains. In fact, the transferability of PCDEs across domains is a very attractive reason to include them as a fundamental part of dance training. This 'win-win' outcome should be used as an important selling point; after all, only a few of today's young dancers will end up on the world stage but all will leave with the skills to achieve somewhere else.

PSYCHOLOGICAL CHARACTERISTICS OF DEVELOPING EXCELLENCE

CHAPTER SUMMARY – KEY MESSAGES

The key points intended from this chapter are:

- A growth mindset fosters positive attitudes toward practice and learning, leads to a hunger for feedback and a greater ability to deal with setbacks.
- Psychological skills and characteristics are key determinants of development and performance across performance domains.
- Psychological Characteristics of Developing Excellence (PCDEs) are the 'hand of cards', skill-wise, that enable young performers to negotiate the development pathway.
- Embedding the teaching and testing of PCDEs into dance training, using formal, informal and procedural structures, is an effective talent development strategy.
- Developing self-regulation skills means performers become actively engaged in their own learning.

PSYCHOLOGICAL CHARACTERISTICS OF DEVELOPING EXCELLENCE

Chapter 2: Commentary I

The impact of this chapter on dance practitioners' understanding of how potential can be realized amongst young dancers is significant, not only in understanding how we can support their development through our practice with them, but also, and perhaps more critically, how we can foster self-regulated psychological skills to enable the development of potential towards excellence.

Historically, we have perhaps hoped for the best in training our dancers of tomorrow, believing that innate skill and hard work in refining those skills will manifest the best dancers. The nature versus nurture debate has tended to fall to the genetic attributes that dancers come to their training with as the main determinants for later success as professional dance performers. This refreshing chapter accounts for a much more multidimensional approach in the development of young dancers, which acknowledges the role that genetics can play, but prioritizes the importance of psychological skill development in a learning context that builds the self-regulated, resilient and healthy dancers of tomorrow.

Carol Dweck's research about fixed and growth mindsets acts as a backdrop to this chapter, helping us to think about how we might be able to empower our dancers to adopt positive attitudes to learning and dancing. I am sure many of us already employ these strategies in our teaching practice but having them articulated in the context of dance talent development is reaffirming. Simple approaches that promote a growth mindset and enable dancers to make the most of their potential include:

- Praising effort and strategies to learn, rather than commenting on how talented someone is.
- Encouraging perseverance with a task that cultivates problem-solving as a way to influence development through one's actions.
- Staying with a task in order to overcome adversity and promote control.

These quick-to-understand principles have the potential to be easily assimilated into everyday practice for teachers and dance students alike.

Usefully, the chapter provides young people, parents and teachers with a practical toolbox that can help dancers develop psychological skills to bolster the journey towards excellence in dance performance in a healthful way. Suggestions are made for the systematic construction of psychological skills long-term, taught from childhood in ways that encourage testing-out approaches in different dance learning and performance contexts, adapting practices for the individual and repeating the process in order to refine and construct knowledge and awareness. The teach–test–tweak–repeat process is, again, a relatively easy pedagogical rule of thumb that can be integrated into our practice as educators and as part of our everyday teaching approach.

Ultimately, this chapter is about how we can enable young dancers with potential to flourish psychologically, face hurdles with confidence and believe that they can overcome adversity and self-regulate their behavioural skills in optimizing learning in dance.

Elsa Urmston is a UK-based dance educator living in Ipswich, having worked professionally in dance education, performance and making since 1994. She has a full-time portfolio career working in Higher Education at institutions such as London Contemporary Dance School and consulting on the education, pedagogy and evaluation of participatory dance projects throughout the UK and Europe. Clients include Made by Katie Green, Dance Umbrella, English National Ballet, Joss Arnott Dance, East London Dance, BEEE-Creative, Dance Network Association, and Crxss Platfxrm, amongst others. Elsa sits on the Expert Panel for Children and Young People for One Dance UK. Previously, she has been Chair of the Dance Educators' Committee for the International Association of Dance Medicine and Science, and from 2014 to 2017 was the Centre for Advanced Training Manager at DanceEast. She has an MSc in Dance Science and a Postgraduate Certificate of Academic Practice. Elsa is a Fellow of the Higher Education Academy and a Fellow of the Royal Society for Public Health.

Chapter 2: Commentary 2

Overall, this is an informative chapter on the benefits of psychological skills allied with informed teaching and parenting of young dancers. From my perspective, of dancer turned counsellor, the most valuable points of note are:

- The delineation of commending learning as opposed to commenting on excellence of talent, was good to hear and I hope will be pushed forward as an educational tool.
- I wholeheartedly agree with self-regulation and time to reflect as necessities, as setbacks are a part of the learning curve; these aspects were well observed, alongside developing a culture of mistakes as being required for growth.

The queries I have are the absences of the impact of social media and the peer setting, and the language register used by peers and those supporting young dancers.

From my experience, the majority of young dancers starting professional vocational training, arrive with fixed mindsets and underdeveloped skills of the above. A few have begun this way of engaging with learning but most are having to learn it at about eighteen years old. Developmental psychology acknowledges this as a tough time in the growth arc. The compounding issue to contend with is the natural desire to find out 'where one fits in' socially. Many factors inform this decision – what level of talent does a young person gravitate towards (as this reflects self-level in some way), attractiveness, accessibility, shared previous history and a wish to build and test social skills, and the very real pressure of not following the crowd.

Furthermore, there is the expectation of learning support beyond the studio; for example, learning differences such as dyslexia or ADHD. In education, validating difference and supporting ways to make education accessible is more of an issue educators consider, yet the young dancer among their peers do not register this as a promotable factor of worth, as the wish to be accepted socially and liked weighs more heavily. The level of 'differentness' could mean the difference between being easily accepted in the group or being avoided by the group.

Questions Chapter 2 raised for me:

- How could peer impact be incorporated into the research?
- How will this information be available to teachers, educators and parents?
- Although research language is the norm for academia, it is far removed from the day-to-day language reality for many.

There is a fine line that those responsible for early education have to walk: as dance is both physical and aesthetic, not only is teaching necessary, but tastes and preferences come into play. For me this is the dubious area where the over-enthusiastic responsible adult can falter. As judgement raises its ugly head and the clarification of what is good for the pupil, what is good for the school, what is good for the teacher/parent can become fused or obscure, therefore, it weakens the young dancer's ability to make healthy judgement calls (be that self-regulation) for themselves and their future.

Fuschia Peters trained at Arts Educational Schools and London Contemporary Dance School. In 1999 she retrained in psychology and worked for the NHS for three years before completing a Counselling Diploma. Since 2008, she has worked as a teacher and counsellor for the top performing arts colleges and continues to do so.

How can young people best be prepared for an activity, as well as the specific physical elements of talent development?

CHAPTER 3

MEETING THE PSYCHOMOTOR DEMANDS OF DANCE

Introduction

This chapter will provide guidance on how young people can best be prepared for an active and physically challenging activity, whatever the activity chosen or the level to which they aspire. This approach recognizes that although dance may be the physical activity of choice now, it may not always be.

This chapter looks at the physical elements of talent development in domains outside dance and how they could, have been or (perhaps even better) should be applied to dance.

The chapter does make a few assumptions about what might already be apparent in dance, but it also challenges some of the commonly held viewpoints that have inhibited improvements in physical activity for young people.

We are not suggesting that the practices described here are universal, but certainly what has been evident, and still is, across all types of physical training/activity.

The chapter closes with advice for more experienced and advanced dancers, offering insights on how technical and physical development may change with the accumulation of training age – or in plain English, as people get older.

Ways Forwards – Avoiding Simple Solutions

Let's give you a common but non-dance example. At the moment, our society is appropriately concerned by the challenge of obesity and all the health risks that go with it, which is exacerbated by measures taken with younger children, measures that demonstrate that the early signs of obesity are increasing. This example relates to one of the 'obvious and common sense' solutions that are being used to address this issue – the 'daily mile'. For those of you unfamiliar with this, the idea is that every day, the whole primary school (students and staff) get out and run, jog, walk or stagger a measured mile or for a set period of time... say 15 minutes. The clear and simple idea is that, if children are getting obese through a lack of exercise, then getting them into an exercise habit when young is a good solution.

We do not doubt the best intentions of all those involved in pushing the idea, nor question the findings that children are both fitter and even more attentive in class as a result of this innovation. There is a long research record that shows how physical activity can facilitate academic learning. However, our

MEETING THE PSYCHOMOTOR DEMANDS OF DANCE

concern is with the objectives needed and the logic of the argument. In short, what are the exact targets (for example: fitness now or encouragement of a lifelong physical activity habit) and is the daily mile the best way to accomplish them?

In fact, a daily exercise bout is very much a step back into history. Many years ago, ex-military physical training instructors were employed to lead children in a daily dose of basic conditioning exercises intended for general fitness. Indeed, the Scottish slang for PE teachers, 'drillies', comes from this. But does making children fitter at seven years old confer any advantages in later life?

This has yet to be tested, but it certainly didn't in the past. Just look around your friendship group and you will probably find people who, although reasonably active at school age, have now adopted a somewhat sedentary existence. To have the lifelong impact that is perhaps one of the key aims of early stage PE, activity is not the answer. Rather, physical education to develop skills and the confidence in them is the target outcome – impacting on behaviour today and tomorrow.

The implications for those interested in, or taking part in, dance training are numerous. But for the moment, consider this one. Teachers and parents should recognize the essential need for a broad skills base, one that can facilitate competence and confidence, equipping the young person for lifelong physical activity and to achieve any excellence aspirations they may wish to pursue. In short, preparation for dance shouldn't just include dance.

What Is Needed? (Fig. 3.1)

Of course, developing a sound foundation in specific movement vocabulary (graded exams, certain techniques or skills) is important, whatever the targeted activity. However, there is a lot more needed. Importantly, this breadth and style of early activity isn't just

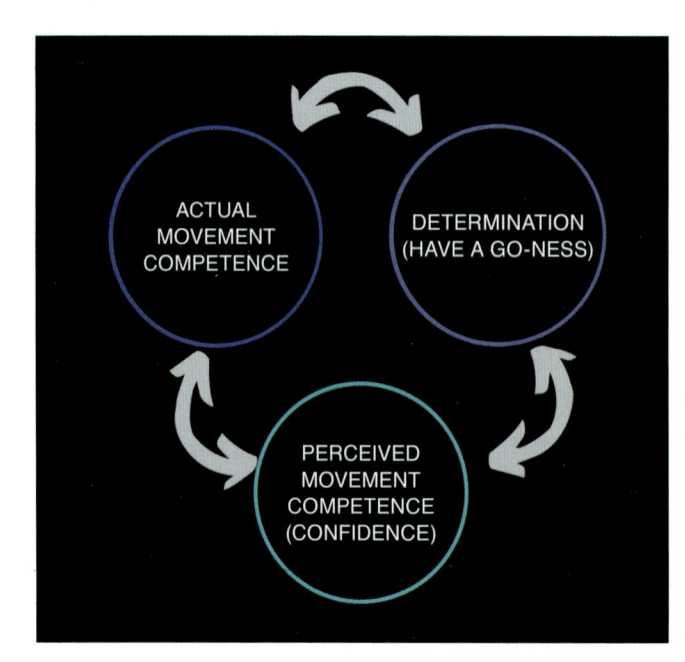

Figure 3.1 The physical literacy triangle illustrates that young performers need to have a set of movement skills or vocabulary to meet movement challenges, be confident in those skills to maintain participation in physical activity and have the motivation and determination to give new things a fair go to prepare for both elite training and participation in dance. Adapted from 'Talent development: A practitioner guide' Collins, D. & MacNamara, A. (2017). Routledge.

important from a health perspective (what authors and advisers call lifelong physical activity or LPA) but also if you aspire to the highest levels of externally referenced excellence or ERE from Chapter 1.

What can research show us about the design, content and approach that can optimize preparation for young performers? Well, the main concept is built on the idea of the physical literacy (PL) triangle, which illustrates that young performers need to have a set of movement skills or vocabulary to meet movement challenges, to be confident in those skills to maintain participation in physical activity and to have the motivation and determination to give new things a fair go, to prepare for both elite training and participation in dance. The nature of PL as the main objective of PE is well accepted. What is also emerging is how important varied challenge in general activity is in supporting its development.

Actual Movement Competence

Let's start with the most obvious feature – actual movement competence. The idea here is that, by being challenged in a variety of ways, young performers can build their movement competence: a set of skills or movement vocabulary that can help them to meet a variety of challenges. This variety of challenges might look like using a different type of warm-up across a weekly schedule, designing classes to include several contrasting activities or using selections of tasks within one activity. For dancers, this means better coordination and more adaptability to different physical tasks. They can use these skills to meet the expected or aspired-to standard, as well as unexpected challenges, whether in dance or in other physical domains, such as sport. In dance, this could include learning new genres or choreography, whilst also being able to perform the more standard movement techniques or choreography for their chosen genre.

There are also wider benefits to developing movement competence: improving the dancer's capacity for learning (they can learn more quickly or be able to transfer skills more efficiently), their ability to take up other physical activities (for example, if the dancer decides to try sport or other genres of dance) and for longer-term health and general lifestyle. This last idea is one that can be used to convince parents and performers of the need for varied early physical activities. Motor coordination is the ability to coordinate multiple parts of the body to achieve an action. In addition to facilitating the learning of movement skills, it also influences physical activity engagement in later life.

Furthermore, high levels of motor coordination in childhood, which could arguably be gained through a variety of physical activities, including dance, correlate positively with academic achievement, and physical, psychological and behavioural outcomes measured in adolescence and adulthood (Kurdek & Sinclair, 2001; Fernandes et al., 2016). Unfortunately, thus far this research has not established a causal relationship; for example, if you become more agile, you'll suddenly ace all your exams. Motor coordination levels in children also correlate with time spent in extracurricular physical activity, diversity of physical activities, engagement in physical activity during school-based PE (as measured by time spent in moderate to vigorous activity), self-rated enjoyment of physical activity and perceptions of ability. Importantly, this association also appears to be enduring, with studies showing that childhood motor skill proficiency influences adolescent physical activity and fitness (Barnett et al., 2009).

Finally, greater movement literacy helps to both prevent injury and speed the recovery from injury (Liefeith et al., 2018). It seems that, due to their wider repertoire, performers with good movement vocabularies suffer less from injury; notably, both the acute (e.g. twisted ankle) kind and chronic overuse problems.

In contrast, effective motor coordination levels in children negatively correlate with sedentary behaviours throughout life (Rigoli et al., 2012). In other words, better coordinated children are more likely to be active.

Clear evidence is emerging that children with poorer motor coordination struggle with tasks of daily living, participate in less physical activity, have higher BMI and are at higher risk of cardiovascular disease than individuals with typical motor-coordination development. As such, developing functional motor skills (FMS) through physical activity (dance) has both payoffs for the development of dancers, and further-reaching benefits in terms of participation and well-being.

Without the experiences of engaging successfully in fundamental movement activities from a young age, a child will likely lack the self-efficacy beliefs (in simple terms, self-confidence) necessary to maintain participation in physical activity.

Perceived Movement Competence

The second feature, perceived movement competence, relates to how good the young performer thinks they are. The point is that, in addition to actual proficiency, young performers need to be confident in their abilities. For the moment, however, recognize that, without the experiences of engaging successfully in fundamental movement activities from a young age, the child will be likely to lack the self-efficacy beliefs (in simple terms, self-confidence) necessary to maintain participation in physical activity. The key message (e.g. Barnett et al., 2009) is that actual competence enables choice, but perceived competence provides the drive to take the steps and persist in the face of difficulty – behaviours that grow in significance as performers get older and develop their skills. The challenges of adolescence make this even more important. No one wants to look silly, but teenagers are incredibly sensitive to peer pressure and perceptions.

Determination

The final part of the PL triangle is what, for the moment, we will call the determination or the desire to 'have a go'. This is obviously important and a feature that is particularly important in adolescence, when concern at looking silly is at a maximum. This feature is addressed in later chapters. For the moment, however, recognize that the truly effective development environment (aka the dance class) will cater for the development of all three of these features.

Therefore, in summary, providing a wide range of activity early on, together with perceived success and the confidence it generates, are important for young performers. Importantly, the benefits of this extend to optimum preparation for aspiring professionals or elite competitors, and to those who are interested in taking part alongside another profession or activity whilst being as good as they can be. This approach can cater to both ERE and PRE performers.

On average, early specific involvement is associated with early success, but not at all (or negatively) with senior achievement in sport. In dance, it is not clear exactly how success early on in vocational training may be related to long-term career outcomes. In contrast, however, early commitment to a performer lifestyle correlates negatively with early success, but seems to have an overwhelmingly positive association with high performance at the adult level. The implications are that later success seems to be built on a 'slow cooker' process: starting early with good levels of challenge, but maintaining a broad base of involvement for young dancers seems to be the best advice, whatever level they eventually aspire to perform at.

MEETING THE PSYCHOMOTOR DEMANDS OF DANCE

Starting Early

The solution offered for lots of the challenges facing children today is to get them involved in intensive training (more than eight months per year), early (before puberty) and to focus on one activity, excluding others. This approach has been the right path for those aiming for the top, whilst, more recently, issues such as the obesity epidemic have led many to offer specialist activities for younger and younger children. There are some truths in these arguments, but the need for early specialization (doing only dance and lots of it, from a young age), is certainly challenged by recent research.

In fact, across activities, early specialization is becoming less common and has been highlighted as leading to several issues. These include burnout, overall and serious overuse injury risk, dropout, poor personal outcomes, social isolation, abuse and limited development, whilst many question whether it even conveys any long-term advantage (e.g. Jayanthi et al., 2013). In contrast, however, and especially for young people who aim to be professional dancers, some degree of early specialization provides the opportunity to master complex motor skills and range of motion, build repertoire knowledge and gain performance experience (for both physical and psycho-social preparation) by the time they would be expected to enter professional jobs, roughly at the age of seventeen to twenty-one, depending on the genre of dance. Importantly, it is also the accepted way in dance, just as it is in sports like football.

Anecdotally, any female aspiring professional ballet dancers begin training before the age of ten. However, we are unaware of much dance-specific research to support or challenge this. Notably, this is certainly not the accepted position for sport in general. Recent literature suggests that delayed entry onto formalized talent pathways within one sport is a feature of senior success (e.g. Güllich, 2011). Partly as a result, success as a junior is not an essential precursor of senior success (Kearney & Hayes, 2018). In fact (and we explore this later), there is strong research evidence that, at least from an 'on average' perspective, early involvement across sports (what might be called general specialization) is much more useful than work in a specific sport at younger ages.

The simple picture is that, on average, early specific involvement is associated with early success but not at all, or negatively, with senior achievement in sport. In dance, it is not clear exactly how success early on in vocational training may be related to long-term career outcomes. In contrast, however, early commitment to a performer lifestyle correlates negatively with early success but seems to have an overwhelmingly positive association with high performance at the adult level. The implications are that later success seems to be built on a 'slow cooker' process: starting early with good levels of challenge but maintaining a broad base of involvement for young dancers seems to be the best advice, whatever level they eventually aspire to perform at. It is important to note that training load overall may be a risk factor for injury (e.g. Rose et al., 2008; Fabricant et al., 2016). Try not to exceed 16 hours of total activity per week, whilst also aiming to provide for a diverse movement experience.

Fostering General Specialization

Putting all the ideas above into practice, 'general specialization' environments for dancers focused on both ERE and PRE would need to hit the PL triangle. Accordingly, a sufficient breadth and depth of dance technique

MEETING THE PSYCHOMOTOR DEMANDS OF DANCE

will equip the young performer for their future choices of direction. Enhancing confidence and the capacity to acquire new skills ('learn-ability' if you like), are also important features. But, against a full curriculum, how can the teacher cater to the movement vocabulary ideas that seem to be so important for developing a well-rounded individual?

General Motor Ability (Fig. 3.2)

These ideas developed in team sports' academies but, since then, have been applied effectively in a wide variety of settings, including dance. A traditional, narrow development of sport-specific motor ability is shown on the left, in contrast to the 'regular enrichment' of a variety of motor abilities (the Christmas tree) on the right. Children often experience a (usually) narrow pre-school and primary motor experience, resulting in low levels of general motor ability or GMA. If they are then 'drafted' into specialist sport or dance training, they continue working in this narrow motor environment year on year. From the activity's perspective, this is fine. Indeed, as a result of this intense and focused training, young performers will often progress and achieve more rapidly than previous generations, looking good early on. The problems come, however, when the young person is asked to perform a skill outside of the movement range they have experienced to date, as shown by the red box. In such cases, the performer must go back to the movement vocabulary that offers some solutions to this challenge but, because their practice has been so comparatively narrow, they must go back (almost) to the beginning. The red line shows this and, in most cases, it is a somewhat significant regression.

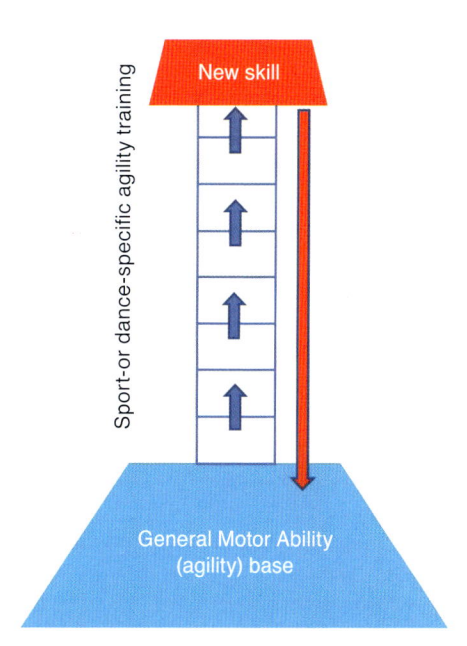

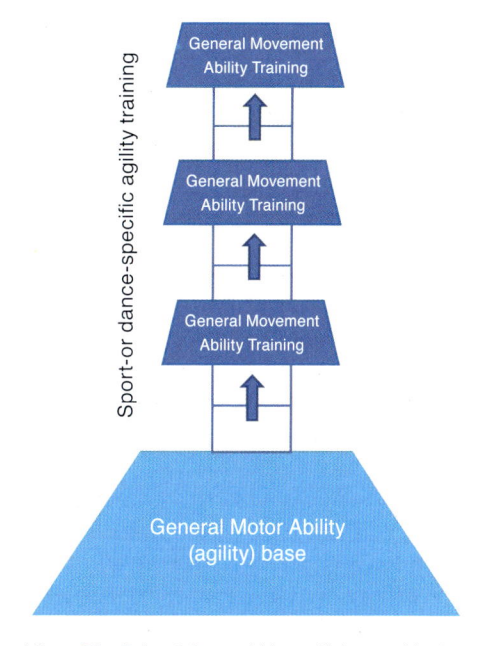

Figure 3.2 General motor ability (GMA) development. Adapted from 'The Role of General Motor Ability and Agility in Sport Performance', Liefeith, A. K. (2019). (Doctoral dissertation, University of Central Lancashire).

MEETING THE PSYCHOMOTOR DEMANDS OF DANCE

Now when we introduce this idea, many coaches and teachers exclaim that there is no problem, as they are only interested in how well the young person does at their activity. For example, if the child is preparing to play football, then when would they encounter a movement challenge outside of their skill span? Well, here is the problem. Even within your own activity (and allowing for the fact that the range of movements expected of, and developed in, dancers is broad), there are at least three circumstances when such 'out of range' movements might be needed.

The first is the growth spurt that takes place in early adolescence. Known also as peak height velocity or PHV (literally when you get longer quickest), this places a significant strain on your control systems as the body struggles to regulate what is almost a different set of limbs. Coordination will inevitably suffer. Educated and aware teachers will know to slow down, refocus on technique and artistic and creative skills, and make allowances and adjustments for dancers as they progress through this phase. A wider set of movement skills will arguably help lessen the impact, both actual and perceived.

The second relates to injury; something that almost every performer will face at some time in their life. Injuries require a modification of control (in fact, a limited movement vocabulary may even cause injury, but that's another story). Once again, a wider span of skills will help the dancer to recover more quickly and effectively, with better performance possible post-injury than if the control span was narrow.

Finally, consider whether styles (and, therefore, movement requirements) will change through the dancer's career, or through changes in companies and choreographers. In any case, adaptability becomes important and, once again, a wider span of control will help.

Given the case for movement enrichment, which is one of the clearest implications of this chapter, how can this be achieved? We could use what we call the Christmas-tree style of programme. This will include two important modifications. First, the range of GMA at pre-school/primary is maximized, making sure that children have the broadest possible vocabulary. With pre-school dance classes common in many societies around the world, dance teachers can make a significant contribution to this, but it will need a bit more than dance to be included. After this, when young people begin a commitment to dance training, sessions are built into the programme that provide bursts of broader experience – shown as GMA training. Basically, these need to offer different movement challenges, with more skilful and talented dancers benefitting from even more 'different-er' sets of skill challenges. Therefore, a typical dance school could factor in juggling and other circus skills (especially good for balance), gymnastics/trampolining/tumbling and even simple team games, targeting this across ages from six to sixteen. Of course, students may be getting this through other activities parallel to their dance classes. The responsible teacher, however, will avoid assumptions and, at the very least, check what their students are doing. As a result of this two-prong enrichment, students are inoculated against many of the challenges listed above; it may even have an injury-prevention role. These suggestions may represent a break with tradition in dance. Changes in this area have been very beneficial in sport, with lower injury rates and less trauma associated with PHV for all concerned, especially when applied to children meeting the growth spurt challenge, which suggests it could be worth trying in dance. Don't forget that skill enrichment during development will inevitably result in a more able adult dancer.

MEETING THE PSYCHOMOTOR DEMANDS OF DANCE

Make performance skills or sequences as bomb-proof, or stable, as possible. Practice makes permanent (only perfect practice makes perfect) and executing performance (movement, expression, narrative, emotion) well under pressure seems to embed the skill, and make it a lot more likely that execution whilst anxious will still be good.

Skill and Training Considerations for More Senior Performers

To finish this chapter, three ideas that will be of increasing use as the dancer nears maturity and even, perhaps, at the back end of their career, will be covered. It is worth clarifying that these have all been tested and proven in sport settings, but have not yet been tested in dance.

Idea 1: Pressure-Proofing Your Skills

Performance anxiety is a major challenge for all performers, and dancers are no different. Indeed, work with musicians suggests that pre-performance nerves can be incapacitating enough that they can impact on the performer's health (Pecen & Collins, 2016). Anxiety among dancers is also high, with general anxiety reported in retrospective studies in ballet and contemporary dance at 50–60 per cent, with 30 per cent reporting

MEETING THE PSYCHOMOTOR DEMANDS OF DANCE

performance anxiety (Laws, 2005). Punishment for mistakes and a perception of the need to improve constantly were cited as reasons for anxiety (Carr & Wyon 2003), and anxiety tended to be higher among principals than in the corps or soloists, and tended to decrease as the number of performances increased (Helin 1989). Accordingly, addressing this as an up-front concern would seem a sensible step for dance teachers and performers alike. We will offer some suggestions on how to cope proactively in Chapter 5. In this chapter, however, we look at the performance challenge and supplementary training as a psychomotor task; that is, how movements can be practised and executed as well as possible.

The process of skill refinement is subtly different from skill acquisition – the original learning process.

There are two parts to this. First, consider the challenge of making skills or sequences as bomb-proof, or stable, as possible. Recent research (Carson & Collins, 2015) has found that working to overlearn or embed the skills is certainly as effective for performance as paying attention to controlling anxiety, through relaxation or mindfulness, for example. The idea here is to practise the skills in increasingly pressured circumstances. Some strategies include practising under fatigue (what is known as contrast training) or by mixing up the skill with lots of others – what scientists call random variable practice. In either case, the performance is monitored to keep things in good order. After all, to correct the adage, practice makes permanent (only perfect practice makes perfect). Executing performance (movement, expression, narrative, emotion) well under pressure seems to embed the skill and make it a lot more likely that execution whilst anxious will still be good.

The second feature relates to the smooth execution of whole movement patterns, like dance routines. Interestingly, the same type of approach can be used. For example, gymnasts will often split their routine into sections, then practise these sections in an odd order. Teachers can be quite creative, using a variety of methods to increasingly challenge the dancer to maintain form.

Finally, even though these approaches are primarily aimed at the movement execution, they can also be used to generate increased confidence, especially when the dancer can watch a 'not up to what I know I can do but still good' performance on video, knowing how much more challenging the practice conditions were than a public performance. Clearly, a case of train hard, perform easy.

Idea 2: Skill Refinement (Fig. 3.3)

The second idea relates to how already learnt skills can be adjusted, in-built errors or habitual imperfections removed and movements polished. This process of skill refinement is subtly different to skill acquisition – the original learning process. Two big differences are the advantage gained by convincing the performer of the need for change and putting the skill back into an automatic/embedded state, so that it won't collapse under pressure. This is called the 'Five A' model (Carson & Collins, 2011).

The important first stage is to convince the dancer that the change is needed. After this, at the awareness stage, the skill needs to be de-automated. There are several ways of doing this but the best for dancers would seem to be the 'right way–wrong way' approach. Using this, the dancer would perform the skill the usual/old/wrong way, followed by the new/better version. With repetition, the differences between the two become increasingly obvious (the skill is now back under conscious control). Now the teacher and dancer can work together to polish the new version. The new version is re-automated by fading out the old version and practising the new. Every so often, the old version is performed just to emphasize the differences between the two and to keep the focus on the new skill, which, by now, feels comfortable, especially against the now odd feeling of the old version. At the final assurance stage, video and contrast training (see the previous section) can be used to convince the dancer that the change has been made.

Technical refinement is not an easy task, but we have found that the Five A approach works well. It is a long job, however – some changes have taken as long as five months from start to finish. Accordingly, it is worth taking time at the analysis stage to make sure that the investment of time and effort is worth it. In several cases, however, the technical change has addressed potentially injurious weaknesses, either physical

MEETING THE PSYCHOMOTOR DEMANDS OF DANCE

Chapter 3: Commentary I

This chapter introduces some excellent fundamental concepts that will support the aspiring dancer to survive and thrive in their training and beyond.

Before you even know you have started, you are already on the path – you might not know where this path takes you, but you are on it!

Unconsciously developing a broad range of movement skills is going to put you in a good place for when you consciously develop movement skills.

If I think back to my own journey in dance, it probably started by climbing on the sofa and then jumping off it. This was probably then encouraged by my mum using the cushions to make a 'crashmat' for me to jump on, and to explore my desire to fly through the air, or move quicker. This is how I probably progressed to jujitsu and country dancing, gymnastics, dance classes, youth theatre, roller skating, swimming, Breakin', cycling, the two times I attended an athletics summer school, and the one time I tried kick-boxing, only to get punched in the face by my brother.

To be clear, I didn't master one and move on, I was just 'OK' at each activity (except the kick-boxing). I enjoyed the movement, the activity, the challenge, the games, the progression, the environment. When I was 'OK', comfortable and confident with one, it opened up the doors to try something else; and this is most likely how and why I decided to train as a dancer; and ultimately travel to many exciting places around the world, working with a variety of different choreographers, companies and makers.

It wasn't this clear to me at the time but thinking back, it is extraordinary how these unconscious beginnings provided a confidence and movement ability to consciously navigate a successful career as a dancer, performer, choreographer, teacher, lecturer and coach.

As a strength and conditioning coach for dancers, I am constantly looking for ways to support a student's development through supplementary conditioning. Initially, to build a physical foundation of athletic competence (such as strength, power, agility, aerobic and anaerobic conditioning), to improve confidence and competence in their movement vocabulary – and this often looks like stepping away from dance technique; sometimes far away. For the students who have a varied movement background, it is often easier to connect the dots to support their movement aspirations. For the students who have only danced, say, a single or a few styles, I have to first create the dots – through play, challenge and encouragement.

This chapter talks about the importance of those dots and the impact they have on young people, students and professionals in dance, and away from dance. It provides some clear training models that can be used immediately, and clearly identifies and describes concepts that can influence a student's training, a teacher's delivery and a parent's support.

How do we improve a dancer's experience and support their talent development, to provide them with the tools to reach their potential, and to empower them to be confident?

I think it starts with the information in this chapter.

Khyle Eccles is a movement, dance and performance specialist and dance-specific strength and conditioning specialist. He earned his MSc in Dance Science from Trinity Laban Conservatoire of Music and Dance, and his BA(Hons) at Rambert School of Ballet and Contemporary Dance. Khyle has also toured internationally with large- and small-scale productions, and a variety of makers and companies. His research focuses on the development of athletic ability for dance professionals, particularly freelance dancers. He believes in developing a proactive, prehabilitative strength and conditioning culture in the dance community.

Chapter 3: Commentary 2

This chapter takes on some challenging concepts but explains them in a way that makes you feel as if you were listening in on a chat between a coach and an athlete or parent. The big words need not put you off reading, as the welcoming approach will leave you feeling like a pro with the basics by the time you have finished reading the chapter.

This chapter explores important concepts that are not yet discussed or understood enough in the dance sector, which is acknowledged throughout, with the need to often cite examples from sport. From my own experience, I feel that part of the reason these concepts are often ignored or misunderstood is because to even begin exploring the implementation of these ideas would quite probably clash with the deep tradition and culture that dance is steeped in.

One topic, in particular, that I am pleased to see being discussed is the emphasis for young performers to experience a variety of sports and questioning the need for early specialization. Too often I see young performers who have specialized in dance since they were around three years old, either leaving during their pre-professional training or retiring immediately afterwards, due to being burnt out and reaching a point where they no longer dance for enjoyment, losing motivation to continue with the rigorous 30+ hours a week training. What is even more saddening is that due to dance being the only activity they ever knew, their whole identity is wrapped around being a dancer and the thought of having an interest outside of dance is a cripplingly scary idea for them to consider. I look forward to seeing more research on this in the future and, as the chapter discusses, developing an understanding of what is the right balance if a performer were to specialize early.

This chapter shares many tools that are understandable and feasible to implement. Furthermore, whilst reading this chapter one can also learn more about existing research, which informs current thinking on this topic, leaving the reader feeling able to make a decision that is best for themselves (or the performer). It also poses the opportunity to investigate areas further, if they wish to, and to feeling confident that their decision is informed by best practice.

The more I reread this chapter the more I want to shout 'Yes!' – this is exactly what we need to be talking about right now, if we are to best prepare the next generation of recreational and professional dancers.

Stephanie De'Ath MSc is the Head of Student Welfare, London Studio Centre. Previously manager of the National Institute of Dance Medicine and Science (NIDMS). Soft tissue therapist at Trinity Laban Conservatoire of Music and Dance. Previously at Central School of Ballet and London Contemporary Dance School. Guest lecturer at Middlesex University, and previously a Dance Science lecturer at Bird College, Canterbury Christchurch University, D&B Academy of Performing Arts, New Buckinghamshire University and Royal Academy of Dance.

This TD process, or the route taken to develop aptitude or raw ability, needs to be carefully planned by providers and carefully considered by able individuals and those that support them to find the right environment and make the most of the opportunities available there.

CHAPTER 4

TALENT DEVELOPMENT ENVIRONMENTS FOR DANCE

Finding Your Route to Success and Making the Most of It

Talent development (TD) is a multidimensional process that allows an individual to turn potential into skill. It is often a formal process preceded by a talent identification (TI) process to enter talent development environments (TDE). The TI process will often include iterative talent selection processes, where students will be continuously assessed and selected or deselected as they gain skills and develop. This is followed by entry into professional or competitive environments. This TD process, or the route taken to develop aptitude or raw ability, therefore needs to be carefully planned by providers and carefully considered by able individuals and those who support them to find the right environment and to make the most of the opportunities available there.

Whether you engage with TD processes as a talented individual or as a supporter, two things should guide your thinking and choices. First, what is the 'success' you are aiming for? What goals will the TD process allow you to reach? (We discuss success throughout this book, but for a more detailed discussion on the differential definitions of success in dance careers, see Chapter 1.) Second, consider what competencies or skills you need to develop that will ultimately support success in that goal (see Part II). Starting with these two things in mind, and continually checking in with them, can provide an important map and constant compass during the TD process.

There is a relatively recent but growing body of academic literature pertaining to TI and TD processes in dance. We will touch on this evidence base and highlight the information that may be relevant further reading. However, our ultimate aim in this chapter is to provide a brief introduction to TI processes and TD pathways in dance, outline factors that talented individuals, parents or teachers can consider, and suggest practical ideas for troubleshooting this crucial process to reach the goals in mind.

Talent identification should be about identifying the factors that can be developed to ultimately provide a successful career: potential for the future rather than performance today.

TALENT DEVELOPMENT ENVIRONMENTS FOR DANCE

The First Step: Talent Identification Processes

Talent identification (TI) is any process by which gifted or talented individuals are recognized, or those with potential for developing skills are acknowledged and given opportunities to develop.

Traditional Methods

TI in dance could occur in a variety of situations, and at different ages and stages of experience and development.

Typically, TI in dance is carried out in a physical audition or observation, perhaps also including a medical examination in the case of some full-time talent development environments. Usually, physical characteristics are observed and measured, including things like current technical ability in dance, current physical ability, including flexibility, joint mobility, movement skills, coordination and perhaps body type, spatial awareness and musicality. Healthcare professionals may also be involved in this process to understand the talented individual's health, injury, stage of development, physical activity or experience outside dance, likely physical development (through meeting genetic relatives) or physical fitness.

Remember, TI should be about identifying the factors that can be developed to ultimately provide a successful career: in short, potential for the future, rather than performance today. Consequently, any TI scenario should aim to identify the physical, psychological and social characteristics needed to learn physical or technical skills. In addition to the physical and technical characteristics listed above, abilities such as focus, creativity, empathy and movement composition can be assessed. In some cases, TI 'select out' those who don't already possess observable ability in these areas, rather than discover and encourage those with less experience the opportunity to train or those who have not yet grown into their ability.

New Ideas

The TI process would be different if it was aiming to identify other factors. Dancers could be observed multiple times, in different situations and doing different tasks that are related to the training or work they aim to do. They could interact with, and be interviewed or coached by, a range of people, including teachers, creatives, peers, and mental and physical health, music, conditioning and academic staff. Adolescent dancers could have developmental auditions reflecting growing and changing bodies and minds. Talented individuals could work on tasks or creative projects or fill in questionnaires. They could talk about their goals, ask questions and share their thoughts.

Debates about which factors can best predict later dancing skill, when and how they should be observed and measured, and whether certain factors are natural/genetic or developed through training, make it difficult to specify exactly which traits may be important to consider in a TI process.

TALENT DEVELOPMENT ENVIRONMENTS FOR DANCE

What is Talent in Dance?

Identification of the characteristics of talented dancers is still in the early stages of empirical study, although, obviously, in practice, talented dancers are identified every day to fill the ranks of the professional performance world, and this process has been carried out in traditional ways for at least one hundred years. However, spotting potential or talent is a difficult task. Raw skill is not always easy to see. A limited amount of empirical evidence exists to shed light on the process of TI in dance, including some information from the perspectives of those conducting TI processes (Chua, 2019), and reviews of the processes and implications of TI in dance (Walker et al., 2010; Chua, 2014). It may be worth exploring this information in more detail in relationship to your chosen genre of dance, or if you are considering a full-time or intensive talent development environment.

Broadly, physical, psychological, social, practice-based and environmental factors are being considered.

Realities of Talent Traits in Dance

As referenced above, there are lively academic and artistic debates about which factors can best predict later dancing skills, when and how they should be observed and measured, and whether certain factors are natural/genetic or developed through training. As such, it is very difficult to specify exactly which traits may be important to consider in a TI process.

Subjectivity

Talent features in dance are highly subjective. For example, speed is an obvious physical criterion for identifying talent among sprinters; however, in dance, ability cannot be measured by a single factor. One dancer may have particular ability to express emotion, where another may have highly aesthetic movement qualities. Both could be considered talented, depending on the person judging or the intended professional outcome.

Heredity

Some aspects that are considered markers of ability or potential ability are genetic (long legs), whilst some can be developed as skills (balance, strength). It can also be difficult to assess developmental aspects in untrained individuals. There is little evidence to suggest that any one individual genetic characteristic is a requirement for success in dance, but research from some areas can shed some light:

> A key debate in the literature as well as in everyday conversation is the degree to which talent is innate (genetic, immutable, static) or trainable (changing, dynamic and possible to develop). As a result of research in a wide range of talent domains as well as our own findings, we propose that talent is a result of the interplay between innate and trainable factors. We agree with other researchers that focus should not lie on trying to uncover some hidden ability or prove whether talent exists or not; instead, we believe that the talent development environment is paramount and underpins success. While the individual is at the heart of this process, it is probably what she or he develops during training that ultimately matters. Dancers with many different backgrounds, training histories, and bodies can be equally successful, and the structure of the training process, the quality of instruction, and the nature of interpersonal relationships are crucial to talent development.
> (Redding et al., 2011, p.68)

Timing

The relative prominence, or peak, of different factors also varies with age, importantly in relationship to adolescent physical, psychological and social development. For example, flexibility reduces in children during times of growth, but it may return once the soft tissues have caught up with skeletal growth.

Anyone who has known a ten- to seventeen-year-old (or been one) can

73

understand the immense change that occurs during adolescence, including physical, psychological, biological and social factors. Accordingly, it is easy to understand how important it is to consider these issues when looking for indications of talent among young dancers. All young people will experience these changes, and the challenge for TI is to be aware of these changes and how they might affect the display of talent at different ages and stages.

Research in the area of adolescent ballet dancers' physical, psychological and biological development has grown in recent years (see Mitchell et al., 2017), although genuine longitudinal research is essential to really test ideas. In simple terms, the best tools are likely to be developed through a process of early measurement with young people followed through to adult achievement by the same people. Currently, we must rely on an emerging picture, albeit that the integration of all the different factors seems to make good sense.

As a further complication, the combination of factors that best predict later success also seem to vary with gender, age and stage. For example, research conducted by Walker et al. (2011) among dancers in pre-vocational training in the UK suggests that factors predicting talent differed across age and gender, including increases in jump height for boys aged sixteen to eighteen and grip strength in both boys and girls aged sixteen to eighteen. However, the same late adolescent group of boys and girls reported lower self-esteem than those dancers aged ten to twelve and thirteen to fifteen. Evidence suggests that there may be a dip in self-esteem following transitions between school settings in adolescence (Coelho et al., 2017); a finding that may be due to an overestimation when young, discouragement when the full enormity of the challenge is realized or, to be honest, a bit of both!

Genre Specificity
Furthermore, keep in mind that the importance of each of these factors will vary based on the requirements of the genre of dance (ballet, hip-hop styles, flamenco, Bharatanatyam), For example, upper body strength may be a key factor for breaking styles, in which powerful movements like headspins and windmills are completed with weight bearing on the hands, arms and shoulders, where ballet dancers would need comparatively less of this type of strength.

Intended Outcome
The intended outcome of TD (is the aim to develop a performer, choreographer, teacher or appreciator) should dictate the TI process. Whether dancing for a performing career, enjoyment, fun, physical activity or a creative outlet, TI processes should aim to identify skills, attitudes and abilities relevant to the end goal.

Chance
Talent factors are also influenced by both experience and chance. A talented person may have access to excellent training facilities near their home, or an experienced teacher may have a school in the town where the talented person lives. The talented person may be seen by a knowledgeable dance professional in the context of a sporting event or social dance event, where they may recommend that person should seek formal training.

Society and Culture (Fig. 4.1)
Talent factors are also heavily influenced by the social and cultural environment surrounding the talented person. Parents, carers and family can support or create barriers to learning or talent development. Societal or cultural views of dance or creative expression as a career or activity can influence the availability of training or

TALENT DEVELOPMENT ENVIRONMENTS FOR DANCE

CHRONOSYSTEM
Life events or larger historical events

MACROSYSTEM
Society, ideology, cultures, values

EXOSYSTEM
Social interactions that affect the individual, but that they do not have participation in or control over

MESOSYSTEM
Interaction between different parts of the microsystem

MICROSYSTEM
Direct social interaction: family, peers, school, activities, workplace, neighbourhood

INDIVIDUAL DANCER

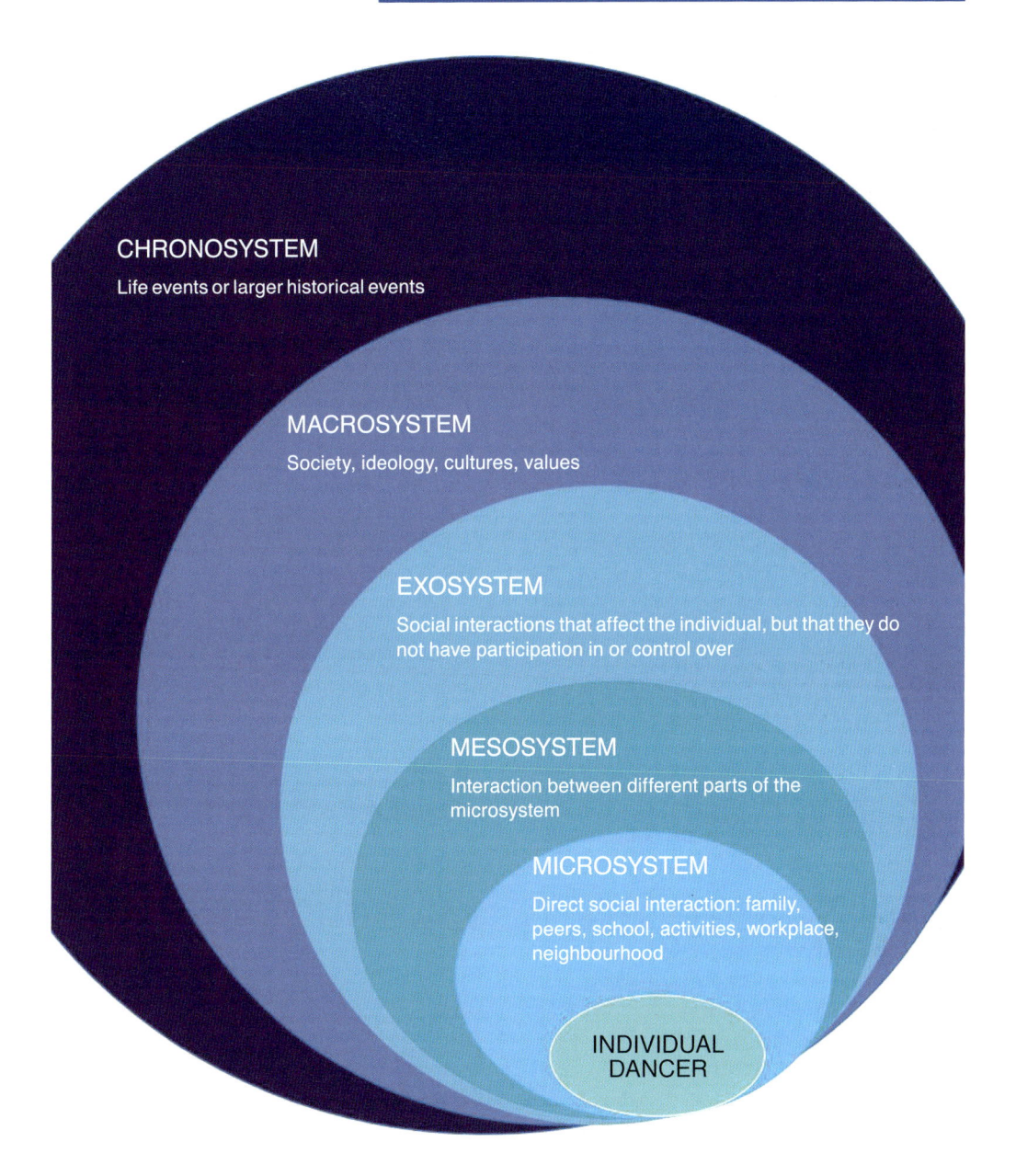

Figure 4.1 Bronfenbrenner's ecological theory of development. Adapted from Bronfenbrenner, U. (1977). 'Toward an experimental ecology of human development', American Psychologist, 32, 513–30.

opportunities. Social and cultural influences might also mean that approaches to practice during TD processes are supportive of learning or not. In dance, families also influence home conditions affecting sleep and nutrition (Pickard, 2007).

Peers in dance influence the decision to continue with training (Van Rossum, 2001) and persistence through training is supported by cooperation and friendship between dancers (Quested and Duda, 2009). Teachers and mentors are of great importance to talent development outcomes in dance as well (Buckroyd, 2000; Lee, 2001). Although students have stated that social support is not important in technique class (Rafferty and Wyon, 2006), teachers who combine supportive and open behaviours with challenging expectations are valued by dance students (Pickard, 2007).

Bronfenbrenner's (1979) Ecological Systems Theory proposes that individual development is influenced by five nested environmental systems:

- The microsystem includes all the individual's direct social interactions, including family, peers and school or home environments.
- The mesosystem is the interaction between different parts of the microsystem, such as the interaction between peer and school environments.
- The exosystem describes the social interactions that affect the individual, but that they do not have participation in or control over.
- Socio-economic status, ethnicity/race and culture are located within the macrosystem.
- Events in the individual's life or larger historical events are the chronosystem (Bronfenbrenner, 1979).

Bronfenbrenner's theory provides an excellent frame in which to view social talent development processes.

Environmental factors affect talent development at both the individual and social levels, as the following two examples illustrate. For instance, a young dancer's family may be unable to afford dance training because their family lives in a large city on limited means and their sisters are at an expensive university. Alternatively, a young dancer may be unable to undertake dance training because their family does not believe that dance is a suitable career. Intrapersonal factors are the inborn or learned personal characteristics, including things like motivation, perseverance and autonomy (Gagné, 2000). An example of their proposed effects on talent development might be the young dancer who exhibits intense passion for dance; practising for hours in the studio and at home allowing him to develop skills more quickly and to proceed to higher levels of performance and training earlier than his peers.

Means

Economic elements can also impact talent identification and development, where training, opportunities to learn, equipment (costumes, clothing, shoes) or exposure to experiences may be costly. Many academics and practitioners suggest that dance talent should be assessed using multidimensional approaches for the reasons listed above. In dance, economic means to pay for dance classes and travel to and from training are also provided by dancers' families (Pickard, 2007). The lack of economic means within the family can act as a barrier to transforming ability into talent (Ambrose, 2003). Talent demonstration in dance is often defined by previous experience and exposure, which may be less available to the economically disadvantaged (Oreck et al., 2003).

Race/Ethnicity

Race/ethnicity may have psychological, physical, economic and social influences on talent development. Beliefs about the appearance of a dancer's body and beliefs about the expectations of the dance world can interact with racial and ethnic backgrounds. Physical appearance and related self-efficacy and self-esteem issues have been described among dancers of colour in ballet and modern dance (Dixon, 1990; Dixon-Gottschild, 2003; DeFrantz, 2004). Codified and performed dance styles have widespread audiences and critics, in addition to the demands of choreographers and directors, who may have expectations about the types of dancers they expect to see when they attend those types of dance performances. During her ethnographic study of student and professional ballet dancers, Wulff (2001), consistently noted that most environments were pervaded by white dancers. This association between a body and a dance style can also be reversed. Brenda Dixon describes the assumptions of audiences attending contemporary and ballet performances by Alvin Ailey and Dance Theatre of Harlem, who believed; 'regardless of style, Black dance is what Black dancers do' (Dixon, 1990, p.118).

In Talent Identification, look for consideration of psychological, physical and social aspects of the talented individual, and an understanding and planning for how these aspects will develop in the talent pathway.

Talent Identifiers

In an ideal world, the professional(s) identifying potential among dancers will have been trained in, and highly knowledgeable about, the factors that may help to predict success among dancers. In most cases, for dance training or education, this would be a team of knowledgeable experts in different aspects of TD, including an experienced teacher or artistic director. For apprenticeships or starting jobs in projects or companies, it may be a teacher, artistic director, choreographer, agent or producer with experience in selecting for the opportunity. Although experience is a key ingredient that provides a great deal of insider knowledge about the demands of the opportunity and the people who have succeeded in the past, more formalized training about what factors to select for is also a tremendously beneficial (but at the time of writing, almost unheard of) piece of this person's role.

TALENT DEVELOPMENT ENVIRONMENTS FOR DANCE

in the studio, or begin to board away from home, the principal of inclusion becomes increasingly important, because dance institutions become their primary caretakers. These children are not shaped in the image of their families, sharing their values and belief systems, but mirror those of their school, their ballet instructors and program directors who are more concerned about their developpés than their personal development. It is important to note that the ability to inhabit a space and participate does not automatically create a sense of inclusion or belonging, in fact the opposite can be the case; othered students often experience cultural isolation and solitude.

(Howard, 2019)

If the TDE succeeds in offering an inclusive and equitable TI process, opportunities are open to everyone on a fair and level playing field.

Dual Nature of Some Talent Factors

As we will discuss in Chapter 6, look out for TI processes that do not recognize or understand that talent factors may develop in adaptive or maladaptive ways. For example, the TI process may select for those who are focused on perfect performance and show extreme passion for dance. However, without managing those characteristics, it would be easy for those traits to become problematic, turning into maladaptive perfectionism (where standards can never be met and the dancer always feels that they are failing) and obsessive passion (where the dancer only focuses on dance and excludes other interests). TI processes should provide developmental support for dancers who may have these factors, to ensure they develop into supportive and adaptive traits.

Defining What Being 'Talented' Means to a Family, Peers and Those Around the Dancer

The implications, possible outcomes and processes of TI should be clearly communicated to talented individuals and their supporters, families and peers. Miscommunication or lack of communication may mean that there is an assumption that TI

There are several ways to gain the skills required to be successful as a professional performer. If formal training is not a good fit or is not available or possible, this is not an indication that the talented individual will not succeed. It does mean that the physical, psychological, expressive and creative skills required will need to be proactively sought and built outside formal training.

processes will guarantee a professional career. Furthermore, talented individuals and their supporters, families and peers may have an inaccurate view of what that career will look like. They may not be told what TD processes may require in terms of commitment, time, dedication and focus, and thus may be negatively surprised or unprepared for requirements.

Hopefully, given the above considerations, you can see what a complex and crucial task it is to identify talent accurately among dancers. However, keep in mind that overall, there is limited evidence to indicate which factors an individual must develop to be a successful dancer, and very little evidence or agreement about when and how to identify these factors.

Key Considerations on TDEs

Selection into formal TDEs, such as full-time or intensive dance training, boarding schools for the performing arts or vocational training, may provide opportunities and potentially open doors to supportive experiences and people that can be beneficial to development and growth in expertise. However, take note of the following points.

No Guarantee of Success

Completing formal training is by no means a guarantee of success as a professional performer and, in many cases, formal training does not lead to this outcome. This could be a result of the possibility that some formal training will focus on developing physical skills, such as dance technique and conditioning, not necessarily psychological skills for performance, business acumen, funding and/or finance, which are all vital skills for a professional performer in a competitive employment market. Furthermore, given that many talented individuals will not proceed to a professional career, formal training should provide exposure to other professional pathways in the performing arts and should instil an understanding of the role that these skills play in the creation of dance performance. This could include (but is not limited to) teaching, academic study, criticism, choreography, direction, management, producing, stagecraft, administration, dance healthcare services, film and photography, marketing and communications, fundraising, and dance learning and participation in community or school settings.

TDEs Accept More Students than there are Jobs for at the End of Training, for Economic Reasons

Look out for TDEs that are more focused on business than talent identification and development.

- Be aware that TD is a costly process. However, you want to be sure that any cost directly benefits the young talented individual rather than the TDE. If the TDE is a business, be aware that their primary goal may be income. It is, of course, unlikely that there would be a sole economic rationale for accepting students into training; however, ensure that investments in training are reaping the desired returns. Check the graduate outcomes, visit schools, talk to faculty, and both current and former students.

- Also be aware that there is a great deal of competition for employment in professional dance contexts; therefore, there is a need for talented young individuals to be confident that their skills are as well honed and developed as they can be.

TALENT DEVELOPMENT ENVIRONMENTS FOR DANCE

Several negative outcomes could follow from this:

◊ In the worst case, a saturated employment market not only creates more competition for jobs for recent graduates and early professionals, but also may mean individuals who have been through TDEs are forced to look for work outside their training. This can lead to the negative psychological impact of not being able to find employment, which can, in turn, lead to self-doubt and potentially crippling negative self-esteem.

◊ In some cases, new graduates may seek work in a field for which they have little or no training, which presents possibilities for new skill development, but requires additional professional development, new qualifications and costly self-funded learning in a new field.

◊ It may be the case that inexperienced individuals who have been through TDEs accept poorly paid work/unpaid work. This negatively impacts their own earnings, but also drives down wages for all professionals. Low wages could result in a poor work–life balance, as dancers work long hours to make a living. Poor mental health could also be a result as jobs are undervalued. Poor physical health could also result with little money for training, healthy food or adequate living arrangements because of all the above.

Alternative Paths

There are several ways to gain the skills required to be successful as a professional performer. If formal training is not a good fit, or is not available or possible, this is not an indication that the talented individual will not succeed. It does mean that the physical, psychological, expressive and creative skills required will need to be proactively sought and built outside formal training.

Talent versus Success

Remember, talent is not a guarantee of success. There are many talented people who never become successful; there are many successful people who have no evident natural talent (though, we would argue that they may have talents in areas that are not being assessed in traditional TID). In the case of commercial success, the current environment of produced and public talent shows conflates entertainment with talent. It is valuable to remember that talented people are not necessarily the ones who are selected to win talent shows just as winning *Strictly Come Dancing* is not necessarily an indication of dancing prowess!

TK

TALENT DEVELOPMENT ENVIRONMENTS FOR DANCE

Positive Dance Environments

As additional guidelines to the characteristics identified earlier, look for environments with some or all the following.

Multidisciplinary Teams Fit for the Primary Outcome

Such multidisciplinary teams include staff dedicated to artistic, technical and (age-dependent) academic education, as well as healthcare and performance support (physiotherapist/manual therapist/osteopath, nurse/medical consultant, dietician, dance/performance psychologist, clinical psychologist/psychiatrist, conditioning/strength coach). All these should be well trained and experienced to support the talented individual to achieve the desired outcome – whether that is a performance, participation, or inclusion goal.

Evidence-Based/Best Practice-Led Training

Based on the recommendations put forward in Chapter 7, check your training environment. They should maintain good connection with up-to-date practices, and ensure that staff regularly receive training to update their knowledge and practices. There should be a clear connection between practice and relevant statutory requirements in your area around (for example) education, mental health, support for children and young people.

Motivation

Motivation involves a drive for focus, hard work, effort and a willingness to challenge talented individuals to achieve their potential by pushing their boundaries with autonomy mindfulness and information. Look for environments that are challenging, but where support is provided to lead to growth, and there is an expectation that hard work will play a role in success.

Goals

A good TDE will focus on performance goals for the future, not for today (e.g. Collins *et al.*, 2019).

Balanced Training Approaches

Ensure training allows for balance between practice and rest, and gives time for talented dancers to develop lives and skills outside dance. This may seem counterintuitive, but it is helpful for health, as well as for performance, to have life balance and rest time. Look at the amount of time dancers spend in physical training, academics, performance enhancement/conditioning and health education. Look at how much time is dedicated to rest and recovery, such as breaks in the day, mealtimes, evenings and weekends. Look at all of this in relationship to the age and stage of the talented young person and be especially mindful of intensive training during periods of growth and maturation.

Positive and Enriching Leadership Behaviours

Any teacher or leader should hold relevant qualifications in education or pedagogy, and child development, *in addition to* training/experience in their specialist area. Updated pedagogical qualifications will include education on safe physical and psychological practices to enhance learning, performance and ensure safeguarding (as discussed above). Augmenting this training, leaders in dance TD environments should create challenging, but fair and supportive, environments for learning. Motivation through fear, or creating insecurity, emotional abuse, name calling, bullying or physical abuse, is neither acceptable nor effective to create good performance or creativity outcomes.

TALENT DEVELOPMENT ENVIRONMENTS FOR DANCE

Rounded Skillset
Talent development environments should aim to provide a full set of skills to ensure employment success. TDEs should create professional performers. Unfortunately, however, and reflecting tradition, they may over-focus on physical and technical skills, missing other key skills such as psychological, business, marketing and job seeking.

Professional Skillset
Talent development environments should aim to instil professional skillsets and attitudes through training including the ability to say 'no.' Saying 'no' to opportunities that are not right for you may allow for more time to hone craft, to care for yourself, to progress personal ideas, and to do work that is meaningful and fulfilling rather than just work. Further, managing expectations for immediacy should be taught. Social media and modern technology set up an expectation of immediacy and a need for reassurance that needs to be understood and managed by those in training.

Physical Environment
Look for an appropriate physical environment for training, education, and development. These considerations will ensure that talented individuals are able to make the most of training. For guidance on the regulations in your area and current best practice, check with the Safe in Dance International or the International Association for Dance Medicine & Science.

In Conclusion

This chapter is by no means an exhaustive exploration of talent development in dance. We hope that this list of considerations hasn't put anyone off applying for, or pursuing, a career or further development as a dancer. Rather, our aim has been to help you make sure your decisions are taken with as much information as possible. Be informed not dissuaded. Discriminating not discouraged. Evidence from other performance domains shows that, even for those who have been cut early and not made it, experiencing a high quality TDE is both positive and transformational.

We strongly recommend you use this chapter as a starting point and actively seek further information in line with the recommendations in Chapter 8 as you experience and progress through TI and TD processes in dance.

CHAPTER SUMMARY – KEY MESSAGES

The key points intended from this chapter are:

- TI should be about identifying the factors that can be developed to ultimately provide a successful career: in short, potential for the future, rather than performance today.
- There is very little clear evidence about which factors can best predict later dancing skill, when and how they should be observed and measured, and whether certain factors are natural/genetic or developed through training. Be as clear as you can about what goals you are aiming for and educate yourself about what skills and training you might need to get there.

continued

- Be a discerning consumer for TI processes – look for and provide open and honest communication, engage with TI processes that prioritize nurturing, supporting and investing in those in the TDE and are staffed by a knowledgeable group of experts employed to support development and growth, and that opportunities are open to everyone on a fair and level playing field.
- Ask questions about how TDEs deal with injury, maturation, change of motivation or health challenges. In the case that a change occurs, the TI process should be agile and well prepared to support the talented individual to engage with the change/challenge and make the best choice for their future.
- Avoid environments where tradition goes unquestioned, e.g. (physical) factors are the only indicators of potential in dance.
- Completing formal training is by no means a guarantee of success as a professional performer and, in many cases, formal training does not lead to this outcome. There are several ways to gain the skills required to be successful as a professional performer.

TK

CHAPTER 5

PARENTING AND SUPPORTING THE PERFORMER – MENTAL CHALLENGES ALONG THE PATHWAY

Welfare, Health and Illness

Getting a Perspective on Mental Health

It is important to have an informed perspective on mental health, and it is extremely positive to see this topic gaining (at last) a level of attention reflecting its importance. Figures vary across commentators or sources but, as a rough guide, about a third of us will experience a mental issue some time in our lives that should be referred to a specialist provider: counsellor, clinical psychologist or psychiatrist. Couple this with the fact that half of these issues will have started before the age of fourteen and you can see that this is a significant consideration for parents, teachers and performers alike.

The perspective might seem even worse when you consider performers as opposed to people. Now, of course, performers are people and they experience all the issues that all people face. Crucially, however, they get an extra helping of 'performer problems'. Some might be to do with the physical requirements perceived for their domain (e.g. eating disorders), some with perceived lack of progress (e.g. performance-related depression) and some with the perceived importance of their identity as a performer, which locks almost every element of their being to their progress and performance in dance. Note that perception is a common element here; this will be vitally important as you will see through this chapter. In any case, the challenges seem rather large, with person problems and performer problems combined with the risks of mental illness to represent a concern or, for some, even a threat, to their career and health.

However, mental health issues (MHIs) are not rare and can be extremely significant and impactful; but they need not necessarily be either. Indeed, given that any area of endeavour (like trying to be a good performer) is likely to involve some stress and strain, bringing a proactive approach, where possible, to meeting these formidable challenges is likely to benefit both the performer and the person.

MHIs in Performance Domains

There are a few qualifiers that need to be stressed to really get a handle on MHIs in performance domains. Many of the points here are taken from an open access paper by Lebrun and Collins (2017). Although the paper is focused on high-level sport, our ongoing work highlights that virtually all the issues the paper describes do apply across other performance domains, including dance.

The first is to consider the plus point of being a performer. Performers are peculiar in both a negative (performer problems, as described above) but also a positive way, namely performer skills. Getting to the top in anything requires a good level of several mental skills, a feature covered in Chapter 2 as the Psychological Characteristics for Developing Excellence (PCDEs). This means that performers have often learnt and got confident/comfortable with a range of mental skills, which would be effective in addressing challenges outside the dance world as well as in it. As an added feature (cf. Chapter 2) they will have also developed the PCDE skill of seeking and using social support, making them more likely to seek appropriate help; often an essential, especially if the MHI is severe. The only issue here is that, as a frustratingly common human trait, people often compartmentalize their knowledge: 'I learnt that here, so it's only useful here'. Consequently, it is important to develop skills across areas and encourage adaptability by stressing how an adaptive and transferable approach can be developed for each challenge.

A second consideration is to recognize and allow for the different levels of MHI; something that recent work suggests people may find hard to do. Think of a parallel physical illness continuum: from a twisted ankle, through a grade 2 hamstring tear, to malignant cancer. Each will require different levels of concern and different levels of specialist practitioner support. In similar fashion, it is important to recognize and cater for 'ups and downs' in mood (rather too common in even the most positive of people, especially adolescents), against something acute or transient, such as disordered eating or mild depression, against a much more serious issue, such as an eating disorder, severe depression or a personality disorder. Genetic influences on conditions are also important here and recognizing a trait in parents or siblings is a factor worthy of note and even, perhaps, proactive attention.

The third factor comes back to perception. For a start, it is important to recognize that many performance domains involve patterns of behaviour that, for others, would be considered dysfunctional. For example, most top performers would score on metrics as mildly obsessive–compulsive, display mild bouts of short-term depression and have a very different viewpoint as to what represents a balanced lifestyle. The point here is that, whilst it is always important to check if something you see concerns you, there are lots of peculiarities to top performers (and those who aspire to that status), only some or perhaps almost none of which will be genuinely dysfunctional. As a silly (but accurate) example, becoming a sumo wrestler involves almost the necessity of disordered eating, at least as compared to your average person. Of course, if you keep following that behaviour after you retire, then that may well be rather dysfunctional and merit attention. The point here is to consider different perceptions and what is normal, rational and medically OK before you pitch in to help.

Finally, and against the caveats offered in this section, it is always important to check that all is well, actually and perceptually, with what you see happening or suspect might be. Early intervention and a proactive approach both work well with MHIs of all levels and descriptions. Thus, generating and playing a part in an environment that sees no stigma attached to MHIs, will be vital in maintaining a welfare-focus (cf. Hill *et al.*, 2015; Gulliver, 2017).

PARENTING AND SUPPORTING THE PERFORMER

Performers have often learnt a range of mental skills that would be effective in addressing challenges outside the dance world as well as in it, such as seeking and using social support, making them more likely to seek appropriate help.

The Crucial Trio: Preparation, Challenge and Positivity

Building from the ideas above, in tandem with the rest of the content in this book, how can you, as performer, teacher, parent or company director, ensure that mental welfare is addressed whilst progress is optimized? Well, here are a few ideas that have worked well for us in other performance domains.

Preparation – Developing and Embedding Skills (Fig. 5.1)

One of the many frustrations of a performance psychologist is that many people (and not a few practitioners) see them as working to a medical model. That is, rather like a GP, you come to see them when something isn't right, or even leave it till the wheels are almost off. Clearly, there is a role for psychological help to address emerging issues, of varying severity. However, any good practitioner will see their work as carrying a proactive element, especially with developing performers, and incorporate ideas, skills and attitudes that prepare the performer for challenges to come. One way of thinking about how to do this is the nested approach. Teachers or parents will do things to address today's challenge, be it learning a movement or routine or preparing for a performance; usually known as micro factors. But, as longer-term, higher-order considerations, they will also have agendas for how the performer is to be developed over the intermediate (meso) and longer term (macro). This means that decision-making about planning classes, dealing with challenges that arise day to day and debriefing/reviewing to tweak things going forward, will all have a nested (fitting into each other like Russian dolls) planning drive (cf. Abraham & Collins, 2011).

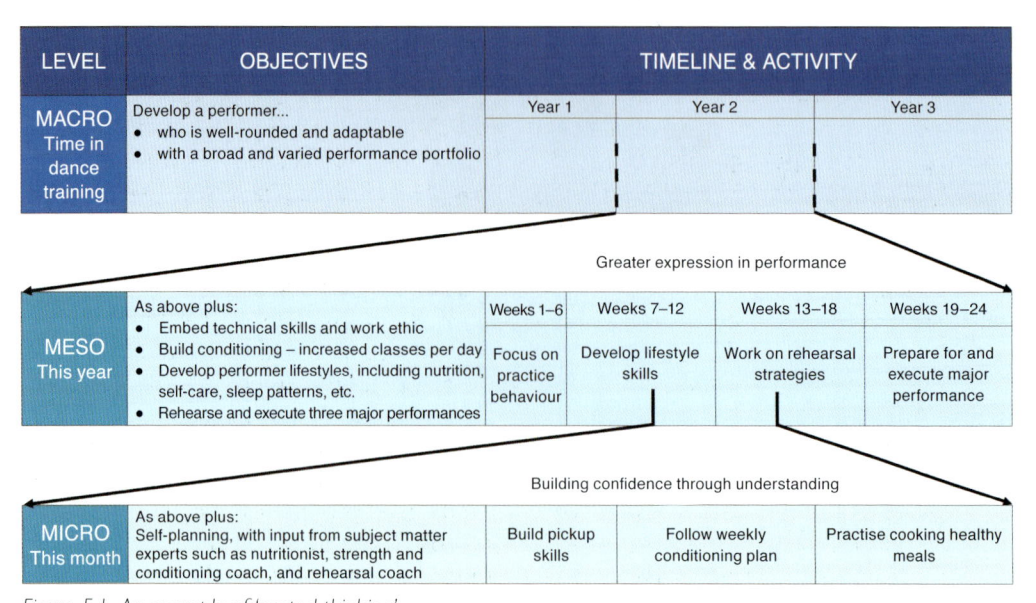

LEVEL	OBJECTIVES	TIMELINE & ACTIVITY			
MACRO Time in dance training	Develop a performer... • who is well-rounded and adaptable • with a broad and varied performance portfolio	Year 1	Year 2		Year 3
	Greater expression in performance				
MESO This year	As above plus: • Embed technical skills and work ethic • Build conditioning – increased classes per day • Develop performer lifestyles, including nutrition, self-care, sleep patterns, etc. • Rehearse and execute three major performances	Weeks 1–6 Focus on practice behaviour	Weeks 7–12 Develop lifestyle skills	Weeks 13–18 Work on rehearsal strategies	Weeks 19–24 Prepare for and execute major performance
	Building confidence through understanding				
MICRO This month	As above plus: Self-planning, with input from subject matter experts such as nutritionist, strength and conditioning coach, and rehearsal coach	Build pickup skills	Follow weekly conditioning plan		Practise cooking healthy meals

Figure 5.1 An example of 'nested thinking'.

These different-level agendas can be driven by a variety of approaches. For example, performers may be encouraged to keep a mental or written record of corrections, reflections on challenges and successes, and/or tasks and skills learned. This record may help with day-to-day memory and tracking short-term progress, but it also helps dance students learn to attend to their own progress, to set and track their own goals and to notice where progress is or isn't happening. This is a key skill for professional careers where individual feedback from teachers, coaches and audition panels may be limited.

As a simple example, consider a parent who encourages basic politeness in their child. Of course, it might be pleasant to hear please and thank you as a learned response. However, there are some longer-term aims in developing this simple habit – things that will contribute to a productive and socially powerful pattern of behaviour years later.

Sensible development agendas will think ahead: developing and establishing skills as a part of the performer's repertoire that will serve a purpose later, then building their confidence in using the skills in adaptable ways to generate bespoke packages designed to address specific challenges. Under this approach, challenges that come up in the future are considered as natural, inevitable and even supportive of growth – and preparation for them is proactive.

Challenge – Avoiding Habits and Staying Adaptable

Once again, building from the ideas presented elsewhere in this book, it is worth acknowledging that progress, towards becoming a top professional or just getting better, is achieved through overcoming a series of challenges. As described in Chapter 2, the sequence of teach–test–tweak–repeat (TTTR) is an integral part of peoples' development of dance and development of themselves through dance. As such, all performers should recognize, accept and even embrace the idea that progression will inherently involve overcoming challenges, even if overcoming some of them might take a while and/or be a real stretch. Recognizing this, and building on the nested practice idea described above, teachers and parents can collaborate/mutually support each other as the performer moves, mostly/eventually successfully, through the progressive steps. These will sometimes be planned or sometimes just take advantage of naturally occurring challenges, such as exams, changing schools and social interactions.

In fact, offering a set of diverse challenges, whilst also preparing for these specifically (e.g. how should we best prepare for…) and generically (have you read X's biography where they faced…? How could they have done that better? How would we work together to…?) is a big part of how a talent development environment (TDE) is best constructed. The variety offers trainees the opportunity to transfer and adapt their growing skillset; this builds confidence and develops the skills of coping with challenges, both expected and unexpected.

Habitual Coping Styles

One thing to watch for is a habitual approach to challenge, even if it seems to be working in the short term. There is a lovely expression on habit from Samuel Johnson: 'The chains of habit are too weak to be felt until they are too strong to be broken' (originally 1748 – see Hawkins, 2011). Whilst developing a habit of positivity and proactive action is mostly a good idea (cf. the 'Thinking Positive – Rational Optimism NOT Blind Faith' section), the performer also must build a recognition that sometimes their habitual approach can be counterproductive.

Coping style is a great example of this. Most sports and high-challenge/high-pressure work environments explicitly favour an approach where the individual immediately focuses on a solution to the challenge. This solution-focused approach features heavily in military, police and stockbroking/sales' environments. Not entirely causative, but there is no doubt that many issues, interpersonal ones are a good case in point, do not react well to a 'come on then, let's get this sorted' approach. The alternative style, termed emotion-focused coping (dealing with what the problem does to you, rather than the problem itself) was developed in association with a typically insurmountable (for most of those involved) challenge, having a family member with severe cancer. In this case, family members may end up 'churning on empty', trying to sort a problem that, for them at least, is unsortable. Therefore, the point here is that, even if the particular social setting encourages a specific approach (to be stereotypic, solution for rugby players, emotion for performers) and/or an individual habitually tends to an approach, teachers and parents should encourage adaptability, leading to 'flexible copers'.

Pushing this through the tweak stage of our TTTR model is one way to do this; for example, when a certain approach isn't working, changing approach early and often until something does work. Offering a role model of using different approaches is another, and making use of various challenges (and discussion around them) to encourage a wider repertoire of coping styles, are all features of good TDEs that fully exploit the challenge idea. Thus, teachers, parents or even peers can point to how others have coped with the same problem that the performer is experiencing. Talking about what 'they are feeling and doing' is a really useful way to suggest alternatives and can also give you some additional clues as to what the performer is thinking, as they tend to project their own experiences and feelings to explain how they see others handling the challenge.

Anticipation
Another way to think about coping is in terms of when it occurs. Most people think of coping behaviours following challenge experiences; for example, you cope with a stress that is already happening. However, key to successful management of performer and people problems is being prepared for challenges you can anticipate, as we have said already. Knowing what challenges performers typically experience, both broadly and specific to your context, can help you build and practise skills to support your development. However, another key to coping before a challenge is the fundamental realization that challenges that arise in the future are natural, inevitable, necessary and supportive of growth. Challenge is a good thing, and it shouldn't be something to fear, worry over or avoid. This way of thinking about coping is known as proactive coping, a future-focused activity to reappraise the way challenges are viewed (as a route towards growth), and to cope with these positive challenges by setting goals and planning (for more information, see: Greenglass & Fiksenbaum 2009).

Thinking Positive – Rational Optimism Not Blind Faith
We are already on record as suggesting that 'talent needs trauma' (cf. Collins & MacNamara, 2012), albeit that this trauma

PARENTING AND SUPPORTING THE PERFORMER

Making of the cover of this book. A lot of planning goes into making a 'leap of faith'. As Winston Churchill said 'I am an optimist. It does not seem too much use being anything else' (Churchill, 2014).

is almost always the disappointment of underachieving (and the spur that this should provide to greater efforts), rather than chasing someone with a baseball bat. Importantly, however, even given the emphasis above on the use of challenge and the almost inevitable experience of disappointment, healthy, developing performers will generally be buoyed by a sense of optimism. Being generally happy with one's lot in life is a feature of welfare.

For example, the psychiatrist and psychologist Raj Persaud (1997) suggests that, on average, people should rate their happiness as 7/10 (10 high). Score consistently 10, and something is likely to go wrong soon (unless you are an incredibly sorted and lucky person), whilst consistently low scores are always worth investigating.

Such an attitude should be developed (see: Seligman, 1991) as a rational act, not just trusting to luck. Seligman (2011) later extended these ideas from positive psychology to develop his PERMA model. All these elements can be addressed to be part of effective TDEs, classes and quality teaching. The five factors, plus some dance examples, are as follows.

P – Positive Emotion

Positive emotions will flow from an optimistic view of life, plus experiencing genuine enjoyment in one's life experiences. Accordingly, presenting a 'can do/can solve' to challenges, where appropriate (i.e. the solution is possible and in your own control – not 'world peace'), and encouraging real pleasure in achievement and taking part, will support this element. Positive emotions may come from enjoying music, creative interpretation from a teacher or choreographer, or enjoying interactions with peers.

E – Engagement

You might have heard of the flow state: total immersion in an activity where time just flies by (Csikszentmihalyi, 2008). This won't necessarily occur all the time; even dancers must do some potentially boring routine stuff. However, total engagement and losing yourself enjoyably in the activity is important. If you don't feel this as a regular part of your experience, it might be time to change (for more on achieving this in dance, see: Urmston, 2015). Engagement and creative experiences in dance may happen in performance, but could just as often be the hallmark of being deeply focused on learning a new movement or technique, or exploring a creative task in class.

R – Relationships

Humans are social animals, so taking part in an enjoyable activity with likable people is a double bonus. Mutually supportive relationships are a part of this. Remember that 'seeking and using social support' is one of the PCDEs. Classes and companies where you know people care about you and will help if you ask, are a good place to be in. You might not be friends with everyone, but it is worthwhile (and just plain good) to be interested in, and helpful to, those around you. This will help to 'tick this box' and make for a better environment, whether a focused TDE or a class.

M – Meaning

In our experience, there is a 'spirituality' side to most people, which they seek to satisfy by seeing meaning in what they do. This might be harder to do in your day job, although many try and succeed to find a job with meaning. If you are following a true vocation, however, or a much-loved hobby, it is likely that you will satisfy the meaning element in your life. Try reviewing why you dance, what you get from it and how it makes you feel.

A – Accomplishment

As discussed in Chapter 1, people are involved in dance for all sorts of reasons: some to be the best (ERE), some to be the best they can

PARENTING AND SUPPORTING THE PERFORMER

Making mistakes is inevitable and positive, not something to be avoided.

personally be (PRE) and some for the simple pleasure of taking part (PPW). Whatever your motives, however, seeing progress and having a sense of accomplishment is genuinely positive. Good environments will help you to achieve; good teachers and peer-friends will help you to see that you have.

Finally, it is important to note that, rather than some special kind of experience, the PERMA structure offers the building blocks for a higher quality of life (cf. Seligman, 2018). In simple terms, the PERMA elements should be a feature of any and all aspects of your life. Certainly, something that dancers should aspire to, and teachers and parents should promote.

Parenting and Support

If mental health has become a hot topic in the media, then individuals and companies offering guidance and support to parents is another growth area. Being a parent is a big enough challenge; adding the pressure of supporting your child towards success as a performer is a significant extra load. However, there are important concerns over the evidence base and accuracy/quality of interpretation that many of these sources offer. Perhaps our prejudice is that, as researchers, we always like to see the evidence. Perhaps also, since performers are peculiar, guidelines suited to non-dancers may be less than effective or even inappropriate. This section offers a few thoughts on what has proven useful in our work with parents of aspiring performers across a wide variety of performance domains. What you have here are some ideas to help your loved ones in the quest towards their goals in dance, whatever they may be.

Making Mistakes

Almost all parents, in a variety of different development domains, are completely committed to supporting their daughter/son, and this support extends across all elements of the experience. Accordingly, parents will empathize with their child, sharing positive vibes when things go well but also feeling embarrassment for, and on behalf of, their performer when they make a mistake, sometimes even when the child doesn't seem to mind. Sometimes, especially when coupled with high levels of desire for success, this can lead to 'snowplough parenting': parents who quite literally push any difficulties out of the way, making the pathway to the top smooth and error free. By this stage of the book, you should have spotted that we think this is not right.

Making mistakes in any high-achievement domain is often likely to be seen as negative, and this is consistent with the perceived culture in most dance TDEs. Mistakes are often met with punishment and seen as a failure to learn or, worse, an indication of lacking innate ability. Not so, however. We (and others) are espousing the opposite idea here – that mistakes are a natural and necessary part of developing talent (also see: Nordin-Bates 2014). Although it may seem good to protect the young performer from bumps, challenges, disappointments, pitfalls and failures, actually, the experiences will afford the preparation, adaptability and genuine readiness for reality as a performer – where challenge is normal.

For both performer and parent, embedded optimism coupled with emotional flexibility (knowing when to push or when to stand back, plus the self-compassion not to beat yourself up because you feel like a failure), will stand them in good stead, whether pursuing a career at the top or just learning through dance. Regarding the self-compassion idea (giving yourself space to fail sometimes or even to give up), you might refer to Chapter 1, where we described the idea of reasonable perfectionism. The ideas described here cannot guarantee an MHI-free existence but, especially when integrated within a strongly supportive and stigma-free TDE, they will go a long way to inoculating against the more severe consequences if they do occur.

Once again, good use of the nested approach in the TDE, plus supportive but 'allow to fail' parenting, will make a great contribution to the developing performer. This does also depend on an appropriate reaction to your child's 'failure', which we will cover in Chapter 6. For the moment, let's consider how the relationship can evolve beneficially.

Changing Roles – Manager to Consultant to…?

Whatever performance domain your child is in, the long road of development will involve several key transitions. Manage these smoothly and progress is assured; get things wrong (most especially through poor timing) and the consequences can be significant.

AN ANALOGY

One of the most key transitions is one with big implications for how parents support their young performers. I am indebted to my friend and former colleague, Phil Moore, from the Irish Institute of Sport for the analogy.

His basic premise is that all parents start out life as managers. They direct and run their children's lives; a quite appropriate relationship, since most kids don't drop out of the womb with a full set of appropriate behaviours. At some stage in their development, however, children tend to seek (and, importantly, need to secure) a level of independence. Clever parents anticipate this step and 'apply for and negotiate' a new role as a consultant. Complete this in a timely fashion and things proceed smoothly. Try to delay or, even worse, deny the change, and management might continue for a few years but, eventually, the child-client rebels. Changing your role at the right time is essential, both for your own piece of mind and the efficacy of the support you provide for your child.

Our research on this is currently at an early stage but, so far, we have strong supportive evidence for this necessary change, interestingly consistent from both retrospective and longitudinal data. The same guidelines also seem to apply to the coach–athlete relationship, albeit that a management role can persist for longer before eventual extinction (cf. Collins et al., 2012).

Evaluating Advice – the Key Role of Identity Commitment

There is an awful lot of advice for parents on social media and some of it is awful. One of many issues is where people offer advice that might be appropriate for recreational/low-ego involvement performers and suggest that this will work with highly committed young people coping with perceived failure or disappointment in their favourite activity. The simple message here is that rationalizing the disappointment is both ineffective and, often, downright ignorant, if your child is completely emotionally attached to the issue.

PARENTING AND SUPPORTING THE PERFORMER

> **A PERSONAL EXAMPLE**
>
> I have four daughters of various ages… all are beautiful, having fortunately taken after their respective mothers. Two are past the 'first boyfriend break-up' experience; the other two are close but I can still 'look forward' to the occurrence. Importantly, and even with my low levels of emotional intelligence, rationalizing their immediate upset with 'never mind… plenty more fish in the sea' comments, will not be well received. Both my experience and the literature would suggest that I try to empathize with their emotions, rather than try to talk them out of it. Furthermore, if they don't want to talk about it, then simply, I shut up. In similar fashion, even if I understand nothing about, or even completely disagree with, the importance they place on their chosen activity, making 'well never mind' comments is the height of crass-ness. The point is that advice that might be appropriate for a low-ego involvement activity becomes unbelievably inappropriate when applied to something that is central to your child's identity. In short, ask about, learn and internalize their identity constructs (simply, 'this is what I am'), then cater for this if you genuinely want to support their feelings.
>
> I often think this argument is completely pertinent to the 'life balance' brigade. I have the pleasure of working with a variety of young people, all of whom are focused on, and committed to, a variety of performance domains: sport, music and, you've guessed it, dance. In all cases, they are individually completely comfortable with the balance they perceive in their lives, even if I can rationally see that their desire and commitment to eight hours plus training/practice per day might be counterproductive or even damaging. I must change their perceptions before I can modify their lifestyle. In simple terms the advice is clear. Identify, allow for and respect the value systems of the young people you are working with. Don't just think that daddy/mummy/teacher/older person knows best.

In Conclusion

In concluding this chapter, it is worth highlighting why we put these two important topics together. The simple answer is based on the importance of social support for mental health. Even considering the most severe mental illness (and issues of this magnitude are thankfully rare), there is little doubt that a supportive and caring environment will be at the very least useful in helping the performer. Certainly, research shows that a supportive environment, coupled with the positive attitude and skillsets described in this chapter, are two crucial elements of proactively addressing mental health. The third leg of this stool, avoiding social stigma, is also an attitude to which good parenting can contribute.

The bottom line of this chapter is how much a positive autonomous attitude, something that good parenting will nurture, can serve to promote good mental health. The significant contribution this makes to performance should also be apparent. We would encourage teachers and administrators to develop their own knowledge base on this. Encouraging both a positive autonomous attitude and positive parental involvement will make a major contribution to performer well-being.

PARENTING AND SUPPORTING THE PERFORMER

CHAPTER SUMMARY – KEY MESSAGES

The key points intended from this chapter are:

- MHIs are apparent in a third of the population and, together with performer problems, represent an important area for consideration.
- But a combination of performer skills, perspective, and knowledge, coupled with decreased stigma, can help to counter these issues and promote positive growth.
- Effective TDEs will make use of subtle blends of preparation, challenge and positivity to develop flexibility and adaptability in developing performers.
- Effective TDEs and quality teachers will attend to, and cater for, all elements of the PERMA model.
- Parenting your superstar is a hard task, even if you have been a high achiever yourself. Make sure that you are employing the nested approach to support, whereby your role is gradually adjusted from manager to consultant.
- Furthermore, be aware that your support is for your child, not yourself. What you say should reflect their value system, not yours or what you think theirs should be.

PARENTING AND SUPPORTING THE PERFORMER

Chapter 5: Commentary

I believe wholeheartedly that dancers are predisposed to mental health challenges, such as depression and anxiety. As the chapter points out, top performers are likely to score on metrics as mildly obsessive–compulsive. My colleague, Dr Brian Goonan, frequently includes in our presentations that the same high-achieving, perfectionistic qualities that make a great dancer can also make them more likely to struggle with depression. The chapter lays out this predisposition well and acknowledges that these top-performing dance students are teens and adolescents – a volatile time for even a 'normal' child. But I would add that these issues are further compounded by the fact that many talented dance students leave home to train.

I left my family for a big professional school when I was just fourteen years old. To borrow from the later portion of the chapter, my parents were still essentially managers in my life, and rather than transition slowly to their role of consultants, they were swept out from under me. My distance from them only served to heighten the power of my teachers as the new primary adults in my life. Most teachers genuinely care for their students. But even so, dance teaching is essentially passed down from master to apprentice with little interjection of training outside of personal experience. If problematic or even abusive behaviours were normalized for you as a dancer, you are likely to pass them down without a thought that you are doing something wrong.

The most common reason that dancers and parents reach out to me is to find a mental health practitioner who will 'get' them. Early on this chapter addresses what I have found to be profoundly important when dancers find themselves in need of a mental health professional. 'Normal' for a pre-professional ballet dancer, for example, is not the same 'normal' that practitioners may encounter in the general population. As the chapter indicates, dancers may present dysfunctions that may alarm those without experience in dance.

A mental health professional may see an impossibly thin sixteen-year-old on their couch and begin their enquiry with fear of an eating disorder, but the dancer is naturally thin, incredibly active, and has honed their eating to a perfect science to balance their energy needs while keeping their weight low. This can mean that valuable time is spent on an issue that isn't really an issue because of an assumption, leaving the dancer to feel frustrated and even judged. This is one of many serious barriers that can prevent dancers from participating in treatment or seeking help to begin with.

We must proactively seek opportunities to see mental health regarded with the same seriousness as physical health in dance culture. Parents are powerful voices in this effort, and I encourage every parent to ask what resources are available to support their child's mental wellness in their training. While the question may be met with a blank stare for now, if enough of us are asking it will be heard.

Kathleen McGuire Gaines is a former ballet dancer who trained in the highest levels of Pittsburgh Ballet Theatre School and the San Francisco Ballet School. She is a contributing writer to Dance Magazine, Pointe, Dance Teacher *and* Dance Spirit *magazines where she has written about mental health challenges for dancers since 2009. In 2018, she founded Minding the Gap, an effort to disrupt dance culture to regard mental health more seriously. You can join her at www.WeAreMindingTheGap.org.*

PART III

REALITIES

Dancers and those that support them can use this section to learn about example experiences of excellent performers.
Skills: observation, self-awareness, courage, confidence.

Outcome: awareness of common challenges, understanding of the necessity of challenge for growth, acceptance and desire for challenge.

'For those interested in elite performance, it becomes important to navigate the narrow path between a healthy striving for excellence and the ultimately detrimental striving for unrealistic perfection. This means how to set difficult rather than unrealistic goals and to remain driven without running the risk of never being satisfied. In more recreational contexts where elite performance is not the goal, participation should be more focused on enjoyment and self-development than performance excellence, but it is still entirely possible that dancers with perfectionist tendencies will appear in such contexts and will need at least as much careful guidance.'
(Nordin-Bates, 2014)

Each dancer will face various challenges and opportunities as they negotiate their journey.

CHAPTER 6

PITFALLS AND CHALLENGES

Introduction

In Chapter 2, we highlighted the dynamic and non-linear routes that typify development in dance. Even when dancers follow the same education and training pathway, the idiosyncratic nature of development means that each dancer will face various challenges and opportunities as they negotiate their individual journey. Challenges and changes, including injury, coping with the positive and negative outcomes of auditions, and finding a work–life balance, are inevitable features of most dancers' development. Framing these challenges can be an important skill to learn. In addition, the dance environment presents a plethora of other challenges, including anxiety, perfectionism, self-confidence, eating disorders and pain management, that impact progression and attainment unless they are reframed by the dancer. In Chapter 2, we presented PCDEs as positive precursors to the successful negotiation of the talent pathway. While this painted a strong picture for the importance of psychological factors as a positive intervention to support development, there is comparatively less attention given to the 'darker' psychological side of trying to make it to the top: the psycho-behavioural factors that might hinder progression and development. This is somewhat surprising given that negative characteristics have as strong a potential to derail progress as the positive aspects have to progress it. This chapter will examine the specific psychological challenges to development that have been investigated in dance and provides guidance about how these may be managed by teachers, parents and the dancer themselves.

Two Sides of the Coin: 'Dual Effect' Psychological Characteristics of Development

In Chapter 2, PCDEs were shown to offer the building blocks that enable dancers to cope with developmental challenges and make the most of the opportunities they encounter as they progress in their training. In addition to these positive features, it is also important to examine the features that may negatively impact development. This might be that some dancers have 'too much of a good thing': they are so determined and driven to succeed that they become over-committed to their dance training and performance, and suffer, for example, from burnout. It seems that several of the positively focused psychological characteristics that we presented in Chapter 2 (e.g. grit, mindset and commitment), may also carry some negative connotations. For example, although a young dancer may be performing at a high level, the possession of a fixed mindset would clearly act to limit progress and stop them embracing failure and setbacks as a key part of development. We will return to the importance of challenge and

PITFALLS AND CHALLENGES

learning from setbacks as key parts of development later in this chapter. For the moment, however, it is important to emphasize the need to look beyond performance and ability as static judgements and measures towards a consideration of the dancer's attitude to learning and improvement as key hallmarks of development.

Perfectionism

There are other psychological constructs that are widely considered as positive that may also carry dark-side consequences if present or applied in specific ways. Perfectionism is, if you will excuse the pun, a perfect example of this. Perfectionism is a multidimensional construct that has been linked with both positive and negative performance outcomes. Reflecting the 'too much' idea introduced earlier in the chapter, Flett and Hewitt (2005) describe a 'perfectionism paradox' in that, while dance requires a high and consistent standard of excellence for success, negative and maladaptive behaviours may come from approaching such goals with extreme behaviours focused on attaining perfection. What does it mean to be a perfectionist? Perfectionism can be described as an achievement-related personality characteristic that reflects the compulsive pursuit of excessively high standards and a tendency to engage in harsh, overly critical self-evaluation (Hewitt & Flett, 1990). More importantly for young dancers, dance training involves very high standards and critical evaluation and feedback as part and parcel of everyday training.

Of course, striving for perfection does not in itself lead to maladaptive behaviours – indeed, perfectionism (or at least a degree of perfectionism) may actually be adaptive in terms of energizing achievement-striving in dancers – after all, it is helpful for dancers to strive for, and attain, growing technical and artistic excellence. However, when perfectionism provokes harsh and consistent self-criticism, a focus on negative past or future events (rumination), and on personal and interpersonal inadequacies, it is likely to result in processes underpinning self-defeating and debilitating patterns of cognition and emotion. In turn, these negative thoughts and feelings about self-worth and self-esteem limit performance and progress, as well as (and perhaps most importantly) psychological well-being. In these cases, perfectionism has been found to be a significant predictor of high levels of negative affect in the form of low self-confidence and self-esteem, disordered eating, injury risk, social physique anxiety, pre-competitive anxiety and debilitating performance anxiety (Nordin-Bates, 2014).

Furthermore, in the context of a dancer's development, negative dimensions of perfectionism have been shown to be critical antecedents of burnout in young performers. The key message is that, of course, it is helpful for young dancers to strive towards a high standard of performance, but be aware of the potential impact of 'too much'. Therefore, it is important that these behaviours are monitored and checked throughout development to avoid crossing the line and derailing the development process.

> For those interested in elite performance, it becomes important to navigate the narrow path between a healthy striving for excellence and the ultimately detrimental striving for unrealistic perfection. This means how to set difficult rather than unrealistic goals and to remain driven without running the risk of never being satisfied. In more recreational contexts where elite performance is not the goal, participation should be more focused on enjoyment and self-development than performance excellence, but it is still entirely possible that dancers with perfectionist tendencies will appear in such contexts and will need at least as much careful guidance.
> *(Nordin-Bates, 2014)*

PITFALLS AND CHALLENGES

Passion can be described as having two parts. Harmonious passion leads a dancer to engage willingly and autonomously and is associated with a positive affective experience. Obsessive passion results from internalizing of the activity into one's identity in a controlled way – although the dancer likes the activity, they feel compelled to engage in it because of social acceptance, self-esteem and identity issues, which has been shown to minimize positive feelings and psychological well-being, as well as increasing negative affect, conflict with other life activities outside of dance, and psychological ill-being (Vallerand et al., 2010).

Passion

A second potential dark-side characteristic relates to a dancer's passion. Again, there is a paradoxical slant to this: commitment to, and motivation for, the development process are integral traits that young dancers need in order to be successful. Indeed, passion for an activity has been shown to be an important element of development (Vallerand et al., 2010). Reflecting the 'dual effect' proposition discussed above, passion can be described as having two parts. Vallerand and colleagues proposed a dualistic model of passion that encompasses obsessive passion and harmonious passion, which can be differentiated in terms of how the representation of the passionate activity has been internalized in one's identity.

Harmonious passion is described as a motivational force that leads a dancer to engage willingly and autonomously, and has been shown to be associated with positive affective experience – increased feelings of self-worth and joy, for example. Indeed, being passionate about your involvement has been shown to prevent negative affect, psychological conflict and ill-being.

On the flipside, obsessive passion results from internalizing of the activity into one's identity in a controlled way – although the dancer likes the activity, they feel compelled to engage in it because of social acceptance, self-esteem and identity issues. This obsessive passion – activity engagement that is out of the individual's control – has been shown to minimize positive feelings and psychological well-being, as well as increasing negative affect, conflict with other life activities outside of dance and psychological ill-being.

In developmental terms, passion and perfectionism have interesting implications: how can support and ownership be given to the young dancer to keep passion for dance from turning into burnout and premature dropout before they realize their potential? This is especially important given the various challenges and developments that young dancers must contend with, both within dance and within their psychological, social, academic and maturational worlds. After all, these worlds are interrelated, rather than parallel, and should be managed as such. For

PITFALLS AND CHALLENGES

As highlighted briefly earlier, during adolescence and young adulthood, dance training usually becomes more intensive and is impacted by psychological, social, educational, and maturational experiences for young dancers. Key stakeholders such as parents and teachers need to be aware of the pressures on the young dancer in terms of dance education and development, as well as the extreme influence of the social milieu at that age (Gagne, 2004; Mitchell, 2017a, 2017b). This means that those stakeholders need to check rather than assume the appropriateness of emerging identity during this phase. Positively, if the identity process is 'got right' at the adolescent stage, the developmental process may well be facilitated for the rest of the dancer's career.

example, educational exams, intensive dance training and puberty (with its associated physical and psychological changes) overlap during a young dancer's life.

Identity Foreclosure

As a third 'dual effect' concern, passion may link with identity foreclosure (cf. Murphy et al., 1996). Identity foreclosure occurs when people think they know who they are, but they have not even explored their options yet. Research suggests that young performers who define themselves through their activity – 'I am a dancer' – and have parents, and significant others, who value the activity highly, are more likely to develop obsessive passion. There is significant evidence to show that performers who feel controlled, and who feel that their identity is only in being a dancer, experience higher levels of burnout compared to those who feel dance is a part of a variety of aspects of their life and identity, such as roles in family, friendship and other interests (cf. Murphy et al., 1996).

There are several explanations about why this might be the case. One suggests that the rigid form of persistence found in obsessively passionate performers might be an important explanation of burnout. Gustafsson and colleagues (2011) describe passion as having a 'Jekyll and Hyde nature', with passion seen as both an asset and a risk. Passion plays a positive role in development and it is helpful for young dancers to be passionate about what they are doing. However, due consideration must be given to how obsessive passion can lead to negative affect, perceived stress and various burnout dimensions, especially for dancers who define themselves strongly or exclusively with dance. As such, parents and teachers need to be aware of, and monitor the signs of, obsessive behaviour because of the potential risks involved.

During adolescence and young adulthood, dance training usually becomes more intensive and is impacted by psychological, social, educational, and maturational experiences for young dancers. It is also important to be aware that identity development is especially relevant currently. As such, key stakeholders, such as parents and teachers, need to be aware of the pressures on the young dancer in terms of dance education and development, as well as the extreme influence of the social milieu at that age (Gagné, 2004; Mitchell, 2017a, b). This means that those stakeholders need to check, rather than assume, the appropriateness of emerging identity during this phase. Positively, if the identity process is 'got right' at the adolescent stage, the developmental process may well be facilitated for the rest of the dancer's career.

Potential to Derail: Negative Characteristics of Development

Although there is significant evidence for the positive role of psychological determinants

Considering the inevitable challenges that young dancers face as they progress, it is worth exploring how they might approach various training and performance opportunities. Young dancers who fear failure tend to under-utilize cognitive strategies that enhance performance, such as setting realistic goals and self-reflection, and over-utilize cognitive strategies that perpetuate future failings, such as self-handicapping and perfectionism. Attention must be given to these strategies as a key element of effective talent development processes.

PITFALLS AND CHALLENGES

of development in sport (MacNamara et al., 2010a, b), music (Pecen et al., 2015) and dance (Walker et al., 2010; Aujla & Farrer, 2015), less emphasis has been placed on identifying the characteristics that act as potential derailers of development, or which can even, and more importantly, detrimentally affect the whole being. The importance of examining how individuals respond to challenge and threat – both inevitable occurrences during a dancer's career – is essential for young dancers. Examining and understanding these experiences should, therefore, provide an effective starting point for supporting young dancers as they begin their journey and as they navigate the speedbumps, side-alleys and roundabouts that typify the route to the top.

Managing Developmental Challenges

The pathway to excellence is turbulent and the aspiring dancer must negotiate a range of major and minor transitions as they work towards their goals. Therefore, the ability of young dancers to understand, prepare for, cope with and learn from developmental challenges they encounter will be an important determinant of their development. For example, when rejection occurs, how can a dancer better understand this experience, as well as move forward to the next opportunity with better knowledge and sustained confidence? However, young dancers may often be psychologically underequipped for challenges and, to avoid negative experiences, may engage in maladaptive behaviours that sabotage development. For example, a young dancer may view rejection as a global judgement of their worth as a dancer and a person (reflective of the identity foreclosure we discussed earlier) and may use these feelings to tell themselves, 'I should quit, I'll never get a job.' A dancer who has had the chance to develop adaptive skills might ask, 'Why didn't I succeed in this situation (as I know I have worked well and succeeded in the past)? What have I learnt and how can I improve for the next opportunity?'

Considering the inevitable challenges that young dancers face as they progress, it is worth exploring how they might approach various training and performance opportunities. Fear of failure can be thought of as the motive to avoid failure associated with anticipatory shame in situations where you are being evaluated and has been associated with negative psychological and physical effects (e.g. anxiety and depression). For example, a young dancer may have negative psychological and physical effects, such as anxiety or depression, ahead of exams, an audition or a special class or workshop with a teacher or dancer they admire. Individuals likely to be fearful of failure may avoid challenging situations completely or reduce effort in situations where they are being evaluated, and that may have adverse effects on development (Conroy & Elliot, 2004). For example, if a dancer feels that they are likely to perform badly or appear less skilled in comparison with other dancers, they may avoid that situation or choose not to participate, rather than be exposed to negative judgements. Fear of failure is also associated with stress, anxiety, avoidance goals, emotional cost of failure (experiencing negative emotions when failure is perceived), diminished perception of self and performance, and impaired interpersonal relationships. Young dancers who fear failure tend to underutilize cognitive strategies that enhance performance, such as setting realistic goals and self-reflection, and overutilize cognitive strategies that perpetuate future failings, such as self-handicapping and perfectionism. It is important that attention is given to these strategies as a key element of effective talent development processes.

PITFALLS AND CHALLENGES

TK

Self-Regulation

Given the subjective evaluations that characterize performing in dance, it is vital that young dancers are equipped with the ability to self-regulate. Self-regulation is the ability to observe and manage thoughts, emotions and behaviours to reach goals. Dance training usually includes regular evaluations from outside sources, such as teachers, choreographers or peers. Self-regulation skills may help dancers to plan, evaluate and monitor their own development and learning, rather than being purely focused on the evaluations from others to measure their abilities. Young dancers may also feel a sense of contingent self-worth or that their abilities in dance are connected to their worth as individuals. Self-regulation strategies, such as setting goals, monitoring achievement and recognizing areas and plans for improvement, will give dancers a sense of ownership or control over their progress and sense of development, growth and ability. Self-regulative strategies are needed to diffuse both intrapersonal (self-worth) and interpersonal (social evaluation) concerns. These strategies would help the dancer perceive threats as less threatening ('What will they think of me if I don't perform perfectly?') and, therefore, reduce the need for maladaptive defensive behaviours (withdrawing effort and self-handicapping behaviour to protect self-worth and status). Given that evaluation is an integral and continual feature of the dance environment, developing and deploying self-regulatory strategies should help dancers manage fear and decide may have their genesis, or at least become apparent, during adolescence. In fact, half of all lifetime cases of mental illness begin by age fourteen and three-quarters by age twenty-four (Kessler et al., 2005). This is particularly pertinent to dance as it spans the ages through which formal dance training intensifies and careers are established and developed. And reflecting current emphasis on mental health across performance domains, it is important to identify and initiate any necessary treatment of mental health issues in early adolescence. Given the potential performance and human costs that may occur if potentially serious issues are missed or mishandled, it is perhaps surprising that routine clinical screening for signs of potential mental health problems is not a standard protocol, as is the case with physical and technical testing. Indeed, given the potential damage that can accrue to adolescents through being cut from programmes or failing to progress to a professional company upon completion of their training, there should be a responsibility to extend this screening to those who fail to make it to the end of the pathway.

The Importance of a Challenging Developmental Pathway for Success

In the first part of this chapter, we have highlighted some of the psychological skills and characteristics that both support and potentially derail development. In the second part of the chapter, we now consider how the talent development environment can promote the development and deployment of these skills and how this process can be optimized. This can often present a paradox: a lot of time, effort and other resources are spent in trying to 'smooth the path', especially for those who look like they have the most potential to succeed. On the face of it, there seems to be a lot of sense to this – after all, if outside pressures are eliminated and all the difficulties are 'snow-ploughed' away, the young dancer can fully focus on training and performance, and keep moving forward. However well-intentioned these motives may be, is this the best way to prepare a young dancer for the top?

There is now significant evidence to show that performers benefit from a pathway to the top that is bumpy and idiosyncratic (Collins et al., 2016). In sport, for example, challenges and setbacks, such as injury, seem to improve the chances of success among elite athletes. Indeed, there is increasing attention given to how high-quality and challenging experiences are critical developmental tools. To examine these experiences, we can borrow from research in sport where triads of performers were interviewed in order to find out what the most common and beneficial developmental experiences are. In this study, 'superchamps' were recruited, defined as someone with five or more Olympic or World medals or sixty-plus international appearances, and these were then matched to 'champions' (one or no Olympic or World medals but a seasoned high-level performer) and 'almosts' (successful as a junior but semi-professional or lower as an adult). Their career trajectory was then examined in order to look for commonalities and dissimilarities in their past experiences to see what did and didn't work for these now adult performers.

The first thing that was clear was that the 'almosts' – the superstar junior athletes – were characterized by a fairly linear and smooth ride up to a certain level where, all of a sudden, the wheels come off and they either plateaued or dropped out of the sport altogether. In contrast, the superchamps experienced a bumpy ride and early experiences that were full of a variety of challenges. As a result of this bumpiness, the superchamps had to learn and implement a range of psychological skills; for example, they had to balance differing demands, remain focused and engage

PITFALLS AND CHALLENGES

in goal-setting and planning skills in order to maintain progress. It seems that these early experiences offered the superchamps the opportunity to develop and test the PCDEs and mental skillset required for success. Indeed, although the various 'ups and downs' that typified the superchamps' development may have slowed down initial involvement, this experience gave them a better, more flexible, robust and adaptable skillset that benefited them in the long term. As such, the challenges experienced on the 'rocky road' appear to be an essential part of the young performers' development, as they offer the chance to develop, test and refine the skills needed to reach and stay at the top.

Learning from the Rocky Road

In Chapter 2, we presented the Psychological Characteristics of Developing Excellence (PCDEs) as the curriculum we have designed for developing performers, to provide them with a 'hand of cards' skill-wise, which they can deploy in different combinations to handle the different challenges they encounter on the pathway. However, having the skills is only one part of the puzzle; the dancer must have the ability and willingness to deploy them, together with the confidence to keep trying if they don't work first time round. The environment, including parents, teachers and peers, is also vital in order to help the dancer learn from challenges and use setbacks as an

The challenges experienced on the 'rocky road' appear to be an essential part of the young performers' development, as they offer the chance to develop, test and refine the skills needed to reach and stay at the top.

PITFALLS AND CHALLENGES

opportunity to grow from adversity. A good example of this might be the case of injury – an assuredly challenging time for any dancer, when having psychological skills, using them and persisting through what could be a long rehabilitation, might mean a great deal.

Although it can be very gratifying for parents and teachers (and the young dancer themselves) to be the star and labelled the 'next big thing', it seems that this is poor preparation. On the one hand, this early success has links to the issues around identity foreclosure discussed earlier in the chapter and, therefore, it makes sense to encourage young performers to develop a broader sense of self-worth. On the other hand, an overly smooth and challenge-free early experience appears to be poor preparation for long-term success. An overly smooth trajectory means that the young dancer loses out on the experience of coping with disappointment and how to handle pressure, as well as the opportunity to develop and test the PCDEs they will eventually need when transitioning into the professional world or balancing a portfolio of appointments. Indeed, thoughtful parents and teachers will ensure that young dancers have the opportunity to successfully overcome challenge in order to boost confidence and self-esteem. For the high-flyer who might not experience very much early challenge or setback, this might mean the generation of 'speedbumps' – challenging experiences that can be built in to the pathway to provide high-flyers with the necessary diet of challenge, together with the opportunity to develop the PCDEs they will eventually need at the top.

Of course, for many young dancers, there are already more than enough naturally occurring challenges without having to design artificial ones. Parents and teachers (as we are) are often motivated to shield young people from challenging experiences, and it is important to note that social support is undoubtedly an important element of this process. However, encouraging young dancers (even from a very young age) to take charge and control things for themselves can have positive dividends in the long term (even if it might take longer to get to the solution).

Several methods may be helpful if the dancer is really struggling under the workload, balancing scheduling demands or with elements of performance. From a social perspective, it is important that the environment acknowledges that this learning and struggle is an acceptable feature part of training. Reflecting on earlier in this chapter and the conversation around maladaptive psychological behaviours it is vital that the stigma of being under pressure, or not being able to cope, is removed so that the dancer can learn rather than shy away from that experience. Role modelling (e.g. showing how they handle these situations) within the environment, where older students support young dancers through these experiences, and dancers can seek support from peers or teachers, can be a very useful way to manage this. Indeed, this type of intervention is reflected in one of the PCDEs, seeking social support, mentioned in Chapter 2.

Communication is a vital aspect here in terms of supporting the young dancer through the trials and tribulations of development. Good communication between teacher and dancers, as well as peer to peer, goes a long way to generating an environment where being under pressure is acknowledged, accepted and used as a developmental (rather than evaluative) tool. Of course, this doesn't mean that someone is always ready to step in to help; indeed, given the importance of the 'rocky road', providing time and space to young dancers to learn how to handle different situations is vital. However, teachers, parents and even peers should be on hand to check and challenge progress and offer support where necessary to make the experience positive and developmental, rather than derailing. The dancer should be expected to take control of their future and seek input and advice from others when needed.

In Conclusion

Based on the contentions made so far in this book, dance training environments should consider the full range of factors underpinning progression through training, as well as factors that may negatively impact on development, potentially leading to leaving training, not realizing full potential or, more importantly and seriously, long-term damage to young people. Such an approach should include a comprehensive understanding of those factors that not only promote development, but also promote the required resilience, confidence and psychological strength needed when the dancer reaches the top. This is especially important given the challenging physical, cognitive, emotional and performance environments young dancers must contend with along the talent pathway. Furthermore, given the inevitable turbulence of adolescence and young adulthood, addressing these performance and psychological well-being issues should be an important element of any comprehensive and holistic dance training. Essentially, we aim to equip aspiring dancers with a full deck of cards, psychologically speaking, to cope with the challenges of development and to ensure they can deploy psychological skills effectively in response to challenge and opportunity, and that they make the most of their potential.

This approach is built around the teaching of psychological characteristics of development, together with integrated use of behavioural markers – a shared understanding of how dancers should be behaving in response to specific and general events. It also allows psychological aspects of development to be completely embedded within the development and performance environment and teaching process, with additional support specialist input (from the sport psychologist, for example) when required. Ensuring that the development of psychological skills is a central part of the learning environment is key to its effectiveness; when 'life skills' or 'mental skills' are taught in isolation, there is generally poor transfer and application to dance training.

Finally, given that both professional and developing dancers may be vulnerable to mental health issues due to a number of reasons, including identity foreclosure, injury, competitive failure and other psychological stressors, ensuring that these issues are dealt with appropriately should be an important aspect of the development environment from both a performance (ensuring the best dancers reach their goals and maintain their desired performance) and, perhaps even more importantly, from a dancer well-being perspective.

CHAPTER SUMMARY – KEY MESSAGES

The key points intended from this chapter are:

- It is important to recognize the psycho-behavioural factors, such as perfectionism, passion and fear of failure, that might hinder progression and development.
- Identity foreclosure is an important consideration for dance educators and other key stakeholders.
- It is important to consider how the evaluative nature of dance education impacts on the young dancer, especially during the formative years.
- Challenge can be an important developmental tool on the young dancer's journey.

PITFALLS AND CHALLENGES

Chapter 6: Commentary 1

As a professional classical dancer currently still in the industry and a graduate of the Bolshoi Ballet Academy, I have an array of experiences over the years that have defined and shaped me, not only within my profession but as a person – and I am only twenty-three. Upon initial reflection, these years contained such highs and lows that, to me, they seemed unique and quite isolating; the highs being elating, while the lows almost smothering my career in a blanket of strife and disappointment. Along the way, however, I have come to realize that I am very far from alone in my experiences. The majority of my friends and colleagues can all recount/are going through similar tumultuous journeys that have seriously affected their lives, specifically their mental health. Some have been unable to continue dancing to a professional level; others have successfully graduated only to be beaten down by an environment of poor working conditions and exploitation. And yet others are settled in large companies or hustling the freelancer life, having their resilience tested and dealing with the psychological damage they have undoubtedly experienced to varying extents throughout their dancing lives so far.

The fact that it took so long for me to recognize how dancers' experiences have and are affecting the quality of their mental health proves the urgency of more effective support and development of psychological skills for young dancers. Why do many of us struggle with feelings of inadequacy, uncertainty and questions of identity?

It is, therefore, so refreshing to read a thorough account that not only acknowledges the hurdles facing dancers along the path leading from the start of training to professional work, but also suggests how they can be tackled. Possibly more critical is the transition from school to life as a professional dancer, in which the basic skills required are not included. This chapter identifies the missing links within professional dance training and discusses strategies as solutions. A pragmatic and evidence-based manner is used to outline several points I have noticed as trends affecting a dancer's success:

- Young dancers are rarely prepared for professional life.
- Dancers do not have access to psychological support.
- Deep-rooted anxiety begins at the training level, whereby, illogically, self-doubt and lack of self-worth is cultivated.

In each aspect, the scarcity of attention towards mental health in the development of young dancers inevitably informs the way in which the industry is run, which in turn dictates the requirements and the way in which dancers are trained. There is evidently a cyclical aspect at play here that needs to be addressed and the dancers of today are becoming aware of it. I believe that the time to affect change is now, to build a brighter more progressive industry, and I truly believe it can be done. The evidence within this chapter is testament in itself to the steps that can be taken to effectively prepare dancers in manoeuvring our way through pitfalls and challenges, and how to equip ourselves with the psychological skills necessary for successfully dealing with the art form we love.

Tala Lee-Turton is a Yorkshire-born professional classical dancer and third British female to graduate from the Bolshoi Ballet Academy, Moscow. She has danced with English National Ballet, most recently taking part in Christopher

Wheeldon's Cinderella-in-the-round at the Royal Albert Hall and was previously a soloist with the Astrakhan State Theatre of Opera and Ballet. She is a regular collaborator on photography, film and dancewear projects, while also providing coaching for young dancers and working to address the issues surrounding mental health in the classical dance industry.

Chapter 6: Commentary 2

I work with young dancers in a range of environments, including managing and delivering a high-level pre-vocational course with a group of students diverse in their dance experience and favoured genre. I also see dancers in competitive environments and mentor performing arts' teachers.

Throughout my work, I am very aware of the individual journey of each dancer and the confidence required of them to identify this and to be at ease with it. One of the most challenging elements of tutoring young dancers is to encourage their trust in the process of collaboration between them and their teachers. The chapter highlights that young dancers, especially those who are in demand and show desirable personality traits, should be identified and carefully managed. As a teacher and mentor, I strive to enable my students to find balance and to avoid negative outcomes from the perfectionism paradox discussed so excellently here.

The 'too much' lifestyle is a challenge to monitor, especially in the pre-vocational sector. My regular environment is filled with these types of students. Through tutoring I have learned that the keen and high-achieving young dancer will seek opportunities from many sources and when the dancer shows excellence, they are offered opportunities from all areas. The young dancer, often with perfectionist traits, then feels heightened stress at not wanting to let anyone down and so over-committing to every opportunity presented. I have found that sometimes it is wise to accept that you might have to be the one who releases the young dancer from your expectations and the extra opportunities you can provide. I find myself always offering the dancer the chance to say 'no' as a legitimate response and find regular check-ins essential in monitoring how a dancer is doing day to day.

In my experience I also see students holding back in group sessions, preferring to underachieve than feel judged negatively by their peers. My role, along with other teachers and course leaders, must be to provide young dancers with the information and practical skills to apply knowledge in relation to their process and practice. Often, we can zoom in on the technical development to the point where we lose the individual in the studio and then when we zoom out at performances or assessments, we question why dancers do not project their brilliance as confidently as we wish them to. Joining up technical development with positive language encouraging confidence, choice, voice and personal reflection is a method I continually refer back to within my work so as not to get stuck in the zooming-in process.

I see my responsibility to use the pre-vocational scenario as an opportunity to develop skills beyond practical dance ability, highlight their transferability and to be hands off enough to allow young dancers to become their own selves, while guiding them through the peaks and troughs of their growth. Dance teachers have great passion for their art; this research and its communication in this field are extremely valuable and should be disseminated far and wide to

PITFALLS AND CHALLENGES

support teachers and their young dancers all over.

Jodie Clark is completing a Master of Arts Degree in Creative Practice. She is a Fellow of the ISTD, Associate of the RAD, adjudicator member of the British and International Federation of Festivals and All England Dance. She is Assistant Director of Dance and External Relations at The BRIT School working with the BRIT Trust and a range of partners, including Kings' College London in Zimbabwe and the O2. She has been a Dance UK Teacher mentoring programme. Her previous students have gone on to a diverse range of the performing arts industry including Rambert Dance Company, Dreamgirls, Beyoncé and the recent Disney films Mary Poppins *and* Aladdin.

PART IV

ACTION

Dancers and those that support them can use this section to plan actions, to re-evaluate and edit action plans based on evidence and trustworthy advice, and to recognize accomplishment.

Skills: planning, critical evaluation, self-awareness.

Outcome: effective, iterative goal-setting and achievement based on evidence, best practice, an informed sense of self-worth and realistic knowledge of ability.

Make informed choices and set goals based on evidence, with a realistic assessment of ability, and a sense of positive self-worth.

TK

CHAPTER 7

WHERE NEXT: FUTURE STEPS AND SOURCES OF INFORMATION

Our aim with this book was to present evidence-based guidelines, supported by the experiences and testimonials of dancers, about how to optimize the development of young dancers. Evidence-based practice is the systematic reviewing of the best evidence in order to make informed choices about practice – what both the research and dancers' experience tell us about how to support young dancers as they progress. In doing this, we have highlighted how a systematic approach to development isn't always evident in current practice. On the one hand, traditional practices are deeply ingrained and difficult to change, even when there is little evidence for their effectiveness. On the other hand, some practices are adopted, maintained or discarded without the required criticality or investigation of their value. This is especially true when dancers, parents and teachers are searching for the 'silver bullet' that will help them 'make it'. This might be because, in the quest to 'make it', quick fixes, the success of others or the sway of authority can blindside and tempt. Indeed, throughout this book, we have offered a balance between research and theory, and the accounts of dancers themselves. This is because focusing on the highly individual experience of successful dancers should not be the sole basis for advising practitioners about how to work generally with dancers. Reflecting this, we have been careful throughout the book to provide some of the evidence, literature and rationale to 'interpret' the dancers' accounts, rather than presenting these descriptions in isolation.

In this final chapter, we present some guidelines about how to be effective and critical consumers of research and applied practice in dance talent development – the ability to question the quality of the information offered, the veracity of traditional practices and the importance of not getting caught up in the latest 'hot topic'. The importance of questioning why you should, or indeed why you shouldn't, do something is central to this criticality. We urge readers, whether you are a teacher, parent or dancer, to maintain a healthy scepticism: question everything, ask for evidence about why you should or shouldn't do something, and be the gatekeeper for your (or your child's) development. It is unlikely that in something as complex as developing dancers there is one solution that neatly fits every circumstance; being able to make appropriate judgements and decisions about what is best for you is crucial.

Wading Through the Information

In this modern age, everyone can, at the click of a button, access information about

FUTURE STEPS AND SOURCES OF INFORMATION

almost any topic imaginable. Social media has replaced libraries and books at the forefront of knowledge dissemination and is often the first port of call to find something out. A quick search will uncover advice from how to 'parent your superstar', to early dance education, or the latest 'must do' courses or classes for young dancers. Of course, the ease and speed with which anyone can access information has both advantages and drawbacks. 'An' answer can be found immediately, but the rapidity of the process often stops us delving deeper and looking for alternative solutions. Websites, blogs and tweets provide a powerful and important method of information-sharing and collaboration, but the extent to which the information is evidence-based rather than opinion-based or anecdotal is (at least sometimes) questionable. As such, we urge readers to exercise care and rigour in their digest of information in general, and especially in the absence of verifying evidence of accuracy, reliability and trustworthiness of any claims made

TK

FUTURE STEPS AND SOURCES OF INFORMATION

Being a Critical Consumer of Information

First, consider the flow of information that you consume. Unfortunately, online and in popular books, there is little, if any, quality control and 'challenging' arguments are not presented. For example, when trying to find out what you should do, you can choose what and who to listen to. Often, people listen to those who hold similar views to themselves, or follow people on Twitter, for example, who share tweets about things that appeal to them and block or ignore people who question us or hold opposing views. This self-selection builds up a shared community of individuals with similar opinions and thus information gains credibility and traction: 'Lots of people are tweeting and talking about something, so it must be true, and even better I agree with all of them'. You can also block people with opposing opinions and, therefore, you don't have to contend with conflicting evidence or people questioning your stance. This 'epistemic bubble' is an information bubble where relevant voices have been excluded by omission. This self-selection of information has important repercussions: the ability to circulate ideas that are persistent and persuasive but potentially without evidence is a real danger. Furthermore, this bubble exaggerates members' confidence in their beliefs by not considering a breadth of opinion and information. Pop the bubble by exposing yourself and others to information that you might have missed and consider that against what you already think.

When inhabiting certain environments, whether as a teacher, parent or dancer, echo-chambers can be created where investment and trust of that group's accepted practice outweighs opposing views and ideas outside the group become untrustworthy. Indeed, echo-chambers arise from trusting others too much, especially people that are held in esteem. The key to getting out of the echo-chamber is to learn to think independently and question the information presented. To this end, we suggest that those in positions of authority and esteem have a responsibility to ensure that there is an evidence basis to their practices, the information they share and the agendas they advocate to their peers. This is especially important when consumers of this knowledge – parents, or even the dancers themselves – may be swayed by the authority (e.g. professional standing, accreditation or status) of those sharing information. The take-home message here is that you should listen to all sides of the argument, consider the motives of those sharing the information and weigh up the evidence, before you make important developmental decisions. Later in this chapter, we propose some steps that you can take to support this process.

Accessibility of Information

This brings us to the second point. Given the accessibility of information, how do you figure out what is of value amongst the noise? Of course, there is some valuable information, advice and practice in talent development available, but there is also a lot of less-than-optimum practice and guidance. In this time of constant change, how can you balance openness to change and innovation with the temptation to follow the most popular beliefs of a given moment? Maintain enough scepticism not to believe everything, but at the same time be open enough to incorporate new ideas into your practice. Becoming a critical consumer and having a healthy scepticism is an important first step in how you consume information moving forward.

How to Think Like a Scientist

What tools and skills do you need to think like a scientist and make the best decisions about talent development? Carl Sagan, the noted

FUTURE STEPS AND SOURCES OF INFORMATION

There are many ways to navigate the development pathway in dance – after all, decisions 'depend' on contexts and desired outcomes. As such, aspiring dancers should consider how particular pathways and opportunities support (or hinder) their development. This suggests the need to consider multiple perspectives before deciding which route to follow.

philosopher, describes how easily people can be fooled and then goes on to explain how scientists have been trained to cope with this reality. Sagan describes how scientists are equipped with what he terms a Baloney Detection Kit – essentially a toolkit for critical thinking. Sagan (1995) offers a set of cognitive tools and techniques that uncover errors, flawed thinking, false assertions, preposterous claims, frauds, pseudoscience and myths –

essentially, some very practical guidance on how to work out what is and is not 'baloney'.

The Baloney Detection Kit can be thought of as the tools of healthy scepticism that can be applied to everyday life. Sagan suggested that the kit should be brought out as a matter of course whenever new ideas are offered for consideration; if you are a parent making decisions about dance education options, a young dancer deciding which is the best route for you to pursue or a teacher weighing up a 'new' training development, these are the tools you need to utilize to make the best decision. Often new, or old, ideas are attractive because of who is proposing them (a figure of influence, authority, high stature, for example) or what they offer (the ability to make it to the next stage of training). Even though it is often tempting to adopt ideas or practices at face value, they should be examined for their truthfulness. If the new idea survives examination by the tools in the 'Dance Development Baloney Detection Kit', it can be tentatively accepted and tested in your context.

Dance Development Baloney Detection Kit

Based on Sagan's work, we propose a checklist to help you sift through the noise of the talent development landscape and assess whether you should adopt claims about development.

Look for Independent Confirmation of the 'Facts'

We would urge everyone to ask for evidence and not to take things at face value just because the ideas might be widespread in your domain. Everyone should engage in this thoughtful (and non-judgemental) scepticism, looking for confirmation of facts, as it stops us adopting practices in good faith just because it looks good at face value, it worked somewhere else or it is being promoted by someone of status. Instead, you should ask what is driving this decision, what is the evidence underpinning it and why you should do it this way and not another.

Engage in Debate

As we suggested earlier, people often surround themselves with like-minded people, which, although satisfying, can lead to an 'echo-chamber' of thinking. Sagan suggests that in order to detect falsehoods and plot the most appropriate way forward, it is helpful to engage in substantive debate and consider all points of view about the issue in hand. Listening to both sides of an argument and weighing up the evidence allows you to arrive at an informed and reasoned position for accepting or rejecting a particular stance. As such, keeping an 'open mind' and having some critical friends to bounce ideas off, and engage in debate with, are important in arriving at effective conclusions. Although this type of debate should be a feature of policy development and practice in talent development, this is often not the case. However, even at the individual level, there is great value in engaging in debate about key decisions and ensuring that we ourselves do not inhabit an 'echo-chamber' of opinion.

The Authorities Can Be Wrong

Albert Einstein stated that 'unthinking respect for authority is the greatest enemy of truth' (Highfield & Carter, 1994). Although there are always people in positions of authority – teachers, schools or professional companies – it is important to critically consider not just their status, but also the quality of the knowledge and direction they purport. Of course, 'authorities' can and do make mistakes. As such, blindly following practice because of 'who says it' is not the best course of action. Instead, science suggests that there

FUTURE STEPS AND SOURCES OF INFORMATION

are no authorities but, at most, there are experts. Expertise implies mastery over a subject, while authority is a vested position of superiority. Again, this points to the need to look for the evidence and ask the question, 'why this way and not another way?'. Experts should be willing and happy to offer explanations and the rationale underpinning their perspectives.

Spin More than One Hypothesis

You are probably familiar with the old saying 'there are many ways to skin a cat' and this is certainly applicable here. As we have shown throughout this book, there are many ways to navigate the development pathway in dance – after all, decisions 'depend' on contexts and desired outcomes. As such, aspiring dancers should consider how particular pathways and opportunities support (or hinder) their development. This suggests the need to consider multiple perspectives before deciding which route to follow. If there's something to be explained, think of all the different ways in which it could be explained. Then think of tests by which you might systematically disprove each of the alternatives. What survives, the hypothesis that resists disproof, has a much better chance of being the right answer than if you had simply run with the first idea that caught your fancy or the ideas that are entrenched in current practice. Unfortunately, as we have shown throughout the book, many talent development policies and practices are too often driven by tradition, popular opinion or a narrow view of development. A much better approach would be to have a broader and more open debate, with the different perspectives presented equally to practitioners. How do you decide which idea to keep? Look for the evidence and let the data decide. If an initiative survives this level of scrutiny, it is worth running with.

Keep an Open Mind

We are often drawn to do things in certain ways because that is how it has always been done or it has been previously successful. Sagan cautions against getting overly attached to an idea or way of doing something because it is your idea or something that has always been done. Often, there is over-reliance on familiar tools or solutions and this cognitive bias – commonly known as Maslow's Hammer (Maslow, 1966) – suggests a common failure to consider other solutions. As the saying goes, if 'you only have a hammer, everything looks like a nail'. Essentially, this cognitive bias suggests that people try and make do with what they have, rather than look for better alternatives. Instead, and reinforcing the need to be a critical consumer, you need to ask yourself why you like the idea and then compare it with the alternatives to find which is the best fit for your context at that particular point in time or for that particular challenge or opportunity. This means that you probably need to develop a broad skill and knowledge 'vocabulary' that allows you to respond flexibly and appropriately to different talent development issues in your environment. Critical thinking (as mentioned earlier) is a good way to start this as it encourages you to try new solutions to challenges, rather than always falling back on the same old methods. As another support for developing a greater range, it may be that you consciously surround yourself with 'critical friends' and actively seek out alternative opinions when trying to reach a decision.

Measure Things

It is important to justify your decisions with evidence, as this takes the ambiguity and guesswork out of decision-making. Whenever possible, gather data (or ask others for the data) to justify why you are doing, what you

FUTURE STEPS AND SOURCES OF INFORMATION

TK

are doing, in the way you are doing it. This, rather than opinions and comments (which can often be emotional or personal), offers a much better foundation for decision-making.

Occam's Razor

Occam's Razor is a convenient rule-of-thumb that states that when you have two competing theories that make exactly the same predictions, the simpler one is the better. What does this mean? – talent development initiatives should be as simple as possible, but no simpler.

In Conclusion

In this chapter, and hopefully throughout the book, we have provided you with some of the tools to be an informed consumer and to navigate the information available as you make decisions about the development of dancers. If you want to improve the development pathway and give your dancer, or child, the best chance of success, it is important to put your sceptic's hat on and question what is happening. You want to stay ahead of the game.

FUTURE STEPS AND SOURCES OF INFORMATION

CHAPTER SUMMARY – KEY MESSAGES

The key points intended from this chapter are:

- Care should be taken to ensure there is an evidence base for the decisions made in the talent development environment.
- It is important to be a critical consumer of information, and questioning the why you should, or indeed why you shouldn't, do something is central to this criticality.
- Readers are encouraged to think like a scientist and employ Sagan's Baloney Detection Kit when weighing up information and making decisions.

BIBLIOGRAPHY

Abbott, A., & Collins, D. (2004). Eliminating the dichotomy between theory and practice in talent identification and development: Considering the role of psychology. *Journal of Sports Sciences*, 22(5), 395–408.

Abbott, A., Button, C., Pepping, G., & Collins, D. (2005). Unnatural selection: talent identification and development in sport. *Nonlinear Dynamics, Psychology and Life Science*, 9(1), 61–88.

Abraham, A., & Collins, D. (2011). Taking the next step: Ways forward for coaching science. *Quest*, 63(4), 366–384.

Albert Einstein, in a letter to Jost Winteler, c.1901. Highfield, R., & Carter, P. (1994). *The private lives of Albert Einstein*. Macmillan.

Allen, N., Ribbans, W. J., Nevill, A. M., & Wyon, M. (2014). Musculoskeletal injuries in dance: a systematic review. *International Journal of Physical Medicine & Rehabilitation*, 3(252), 10-4172.

Ambrose, D. (2003). Barriers to aspiration development and self-fulfillment: Interdisciplinary insights for talent discovery. *Gifted Child Quarterly*, 47(4), 282–294.

Angel, R., & Tienda, M. (1982). Determinants of extended household structure: Cultural pattern or economic need?. *American journal of Sociology*, 87(6), 1360-1383.

Angioi, M., Metsios, G. S., Twitchett, E., Koutedakis, Y., & Wyon, M. (2009). Association between selected physical fitness parameters and aesthetic competence in contemporary dancers. *Journal of dance medicine & science*, 13(4), 115–123.

Ascenso, S. (2018, October) Mind the mind: findings on mental health in dance. Paper presented at the International Association of Dance Medicine & Science annual meeting, Helsinki, Finland.

Aujla, I. J., Nordin-Bates, S. M., Redding, E., & Jobbins, V. (2014). Developing talent among young dancers: Findings from the UK Centres for Advanced Training. *Theatre, dance and performance training*, 5(1), 15–30.

Aujla, I., & Farrer, R. (2015). The role of psychological factors in the career of the independent dancer. *Frontiers in psychology*, 6, 1688.

Bailey, R. (2007). Talent development and the luck problem. *Sport, ethics and philosophy*, 1(3), 367–377.

Bailey, R., & Collins, D. (2013). The standard model of talent development and its discontents. *Kinesiology Review*, 2(4), 248–259.

Bailey, R., Collins, D., Ford, P., MacNamara, Á., Toms, M., & Pearce, G. (2010). Participant development in sport: An academic review. *Sports Coach UK*, 4, 1–134.

Barnett, L. M., Morgan, P. J., van Beurden, E., & Beard, J. R. (2008). Perceived sports competence mediates the relationship between childhood motor skill proficiency and adolescent physical activity and fitness: a longitudinal assessment. *International journal of behavioral nutrition and physical activity*, 5(1), 40.

BIBLIOGRAPHY

Barnett, L. M., Van Beurden, E., Morgan, P. J., Brooks, L. O., & Beard, J. R. (2009). Childhood motor skill proficiency as a predictor of adolescent physical activity. *Journal of adolescent health*, 44(3), 252–259.

Baum, S. M., Owen, S. V., & Oreck, B. A. (1996). Talent beyond words: Identification of potential talent in dance and music in elementary students. *Gifted Child Quarterly*, 40(2), 93–101.

BBC. (2019). Ballet dancer Tala: 'We're all struggling to keep afloat'. (2019, May 29). Retrieved April 29, 2020, from https://www.bbc.co.uk/programmes/p07bmz0d.

Beckett, Samuel. 1983. *Worstward ho*. New York: Grove Press.

Bennett, D. (2009). Careers in dance: Beyond performance to the real world of work. *Journal of Dance Education*, 9(1), 27–34.

Bloom, B. S. (1985). *Developing talent in young people*. New York: Ballantine.

Bronfenbrenner, U. (1977). Toward an experimental ecology of human development. *American psychologist*, 32(7), 513.

Buckroyd, J. (Ed.). (2000). *The student dancer: Emotional aspects of the teaching and learning of dance*. Princeton Book Company Pub.

Caldwell, C. H., Zimmerman, M. A., Bernat, D. H., Sellers, R. M., & Notaro, P. C. (2002). Racial identity, maternal support, and psychological distress among African American adolescents. *Child development*, 73(4), 1322–1336.

Carr, S., & Wyon, M. (2003). The impact of motivational climate on dance students' achievement goals, trait anxiety, and perfectionism. *Journal of Dance Medicine & Science*, 7(4), 105–114.

Carson, H. J., & Collins, D. (2011). Refining and regaining skills in fixation/diversification stage performers: The Five-A Model. *International Review of Sport and Exercise Psychology*, 4(2), 146–167.

Carson, H. J., & Collins, D. (2016). The fourth dimension: A motoric perspective on the anxiety–performance relationship. *International Review of Sport and Exercise Psychology*, 9(1), 1–21.

Chua, J. (2014). Dance talent development across the lifespan: A review of current research. *Research in Dance Education*, 15(1), 23–53.

Chua, J. (2019). Talent development in dance: Perspectives from gatekeepers in Hong Kong and Finland in *The Psychology of High Performance: Developing Human Potential into Domain-Specific Talent*, R. F. Subotnik, P. Olszewski-Kubilius, and F. C. Worrell (Editors).

Churchill, W. S. (2014). *The Unwritten Alliance*, 1961 (Vol. 5). Rosetta Books. Coelho, V.A., Marchante, M. & Jimerson, S.R. J Youth Adolescence (2017) 46: 558. https://doi.org/10.1007/s10964-016-0510-6.

Coelho, V. A., Marchante, M., & Jimerson, S. R. (2017). Promoting a positive middle school transition: A randomized-controlled treatment study examining self-concept and self-esteem. *Journal of youth and adolescence*, 46(3), 558–569.

Cohen, S., & Wills, T. A. (1985). Stress, social support, and the buffering hypothesis. *Psychological bulletin*, 98(2), 310.

Collins, D. & Bailey, R. A sporting utopia: easing the essential tension in sport policy. In R. Bailey and M. Talbot (Eds.), *Elite Sport and Sport-for-All: Bridging the two cultures*. (pp. 134–146, London: Routledge, 2012).

Collins, D., & MacNamara, Á. (2012). The rocky road to the top. *Sports medicine*, 42(11), 907–914.

BIBLIOGRAPHY

Collins, D., Abraham, A., & Collins, R. (2012). On vampires and wolves – Exposing and exploring reasons for the differential impact of coach education. *International Journal of Sport Psychology, 43*(3), 255.

Collins, D., Bailey, R., Ford, P. A., MacNamara, A., Toms, M., & Pearce, G. (2012). Three Worlds: New directions in participant development in sport and physical activity. *Sport, Education and Society, 17*(2), 225–243.

Collins, D., MacNamara, Á., & Cruickshank, A. (2019). Research and practice in talent identification and development – Some thoughts on the state of play. *Journal of Applied Sport Psychology, 31*(3), 340-351.

Collins, D., MacNamara, Á., & McCarthy, N. (2016). Super champions, champions, and almosts: important differences and commonalities on the rocky road. *Frontiers in psychology, 6,* 2009.

Conroy, D. E., & Elliot, A. J. (2004). Fear of failure and achievement goals in sport: Addressing the issue of the chicken and the egg. *Anxiety, Stress & Coping, 17*(3), 271–285.

Copple, C., & Bredekamp, S. (2009). *Developmentally appropriate practice in early childhood programs serving children from birth through age 8* (Vol. 1313, pp. 22205–4101). Washington, DC: National Association for the Education of Young Children.

Côté, J., Salmela, J. H., Baria, A., & Russell, S. J. (1993). Organizing and interpreting unstructured qualitative data. *The sport psychologist, 7*(2), 127–137.

Csikszentmihalyi, M. (2008). Flow*: The Psychology of Optimal Experience* (1st ed.). New York, NY: HarperCollins.

Csikszentmihalyi, M., Rathunde, K., & Whalen, S. (1997). *Talented teenagers: The roots of success and failure.* Cambridge University Press.

Daprati, E., Iosa, M., & Haggard, P. (2009). A dance to the music of time: aesthetically-relevant changes in body posture in performing art. *PLoS One, 4*(3).

de Bruin, A. K., Bakker, F. C., & Oudejans, R. R. (2009). Achievement goal theory and disordered eating: Relationships of disordered eating with goal orientations and motivational climate in female gymnasts and dancers. *Psychology of Sport and Exercise, 10*(1), 72–79.

DeFrantz, T. F. (2004). *Dancing revelations: Alvin Ailey's embodiment of African American culture.* Oxford University Press.

Dixon, B. (1990, April). Black dance and dancers and the white public: A prolegomenon to problems of definition. In *Black American Literature Forum* (Vol. 24, No. 1, pp. 117–123). St. Louis University.

Dixon-Gottschild, B. (2003). *The black dancing body: A geography from coon to cool.* New York: Palgrave Macmillan. DTAP: Oreck et. al., 2003).

Duckworth, A., & Duckworth, A. (2016). *Grit: The power of passion and perseverance* (Vol. 234). New York, NY: Scribner.

Duda, J. L., & Kim, M. (1997). Perceptions of the motivational climate, psychological characteristics, and attitudes toward eating among young female gymnasts. *Journal of Sport & Exercise Psychology 19,* S48–S48.

Dweck, C.S. (2006) *Mindset: The new psychology of success.* New York, NY: Random House.

Eden, R. (2013, May 12). Why British ballet is dancing with death. *The Telegraph.* Retrieved from http://www.telegraph.co.uk/culture/culturenews/10051368/Why-British-ballet-is-dancing-with-death.html.

BIBLIOGRAPHY

Fabricant, P. D., Lakomkin, N., Sugimoto, D., Tepolt, F. A., Stracciolini, A., & Kocher, M. S. (2016). Youth sports specialization and musculoskeletal injury: a systematic review of the literature. *The Physician and sportsmedicine*, 44(3), 257–262.

Fernandes, V. R., Ribeiro, M. L. S., Melo, T., de Tarso Maciel-Pinheiro, P., Guimarães, T. T., Araújo, N. B., ... & Deslandes, A. C. (2016). Motor coordination correlates with academic achievement and cognitive function in children. *Frontiers in psychology*, 7, 318.

Flett, G. L., & Hewitt, P. L. (2005). The perils of perfectionism in sports and exercise. *Current directions in psychological science*, 14(1), 14–18.

Fredricks, J. A., Alfeld-Liro, C. J., Hruda, L. Z., Eccles, J. S., Patrick, H., & Ryan, A. M. (2002). A qualitative exploration of adolescents' commitment to athletics and the arts. *Journal of Adolescent Research*, 17(1), 68–97.

Gagné, F. (2000). Understanding the complex choreography of talent development through DMGT-based analysis. In K. A. Heller, F. J. Monks, & A. H. Passow (Eds.), *International handbook of giftedness and talent* (2nd ed., pp. 67–79). Oxford: Pergamon Press.

Gagné, F. (2003). Transforming gifts into talents: The DMGT as a developmental theory. In N. Colangelo & G. A. Davis (Eds.), *Handbook of gifted education* (3rd ed.; pp. 60–74). Boston: Allyn and Bacon.

Gagné, F. (2004). Transforming gifts into talents: The DMGT as a developmental theory. *High ability studies*, 15(2), 119–147.

Gagné, F. 2008. Building gifts into talents: Overview of the DMGT. Keynote address at the 10th Asia-Pacific Conference for Giftedness, Asia-Pacific Federation of the World Council for Gifted and Talented Children, July 14–17, in Singapore.

Greenglass, E. R., & Fiksenbaum, L. (2009). Proactive coping, positive affect, and well-being: Testing for mediation using path analysis. *European psychologist*, 14(1), 29–39.

Güllich, A. (2011). Training quality in high-performance youth sport. Invited keynote at the Science for Success Conference, Research Institute for Olympic Sports (KIHU), Finland 11–12 October.

Gulliver, A. (2017). Commentary: Mental health in sport (MHS): Improving the early intervention knowledge and confidence of elite sport staff. *Frontiers in psychology*, 8, 1209.

Gustafsson, H., Hassmén, P., & Hassmén, N. (2011). Are athletes burning out with passion?. *European Journal of Sport Science*, 11(6), 387–395.

Hamilton, L. H., & Stricker, G. (1989). Balanchine's children. *Medical Problems of Performing Artists*, 4(4), 143.

Hansford, B. (2018). *Building a Dancer.* (2018). UK.

Harknett, K. (2006). The relationship between private safety nets and economic outcomes among single mothers. *Journal of Marriage and Family*, 68(1), 172–191.

Hawkins, (2011) Ed., The VISION of THEODORE, the Hermit of Teneriffe, found in his cell. Cambridge: Cambridge University Press. 145–162. doi.org/10.1017/CBO9781139056502.002.

Helin, P. (1989). Mental and Psychophysiological Tension at Professional Ballet Dancers' Performances and Rehearsals. *Dance Research Journal*, 21(1), 7–14.

Henly, J. R., Danziger, S. K., & Offer, S. (2005). The contribution of social support to the material well-being of low-income families. *Journal of Marriage and Family*, 67(1), 122–140.

Hewitt, P. L., & Flett, G. L. (1990). Perfectionism and depression: A multidimensional analysis. *Journal of social behavior and personality*, 5(5), 423.

BIBLIOGRAPHY

Highfield, R., & Carter, P. (1994). *The private lives of Albert Einstein*. Macmillan.

Hill, A., MacNamara, Á., Collins, D., & Rodgers, S. (2016). Examining the role of mental health and clinical issues within talent development. *Frontiers in psychology, 6*, 2042.

Hincapié, C. A., Morton, E. J., & Cassidy, J. D. (2008). Musculoskeletal injuries and pain in dancers: a systematic review. *Archives of physical medicine and rehabilitation, 89*(9), 1819–1829.

Hincapie, J.C., Cassidy, J.C. (2012). Musculoskeletal injuries and pain in dancers. A systematic review update. *Journal of Dance Medicine & Science, 16,* 74–84.

Hofferth, S. L. (1984). Kin networks, race, and family structure. *Journal of Marriage and the Family*, 791–806.

Horn, T. S., & Weiss, M. R. (1991). A developmental analysis of children's self-ability judgments in the physical domain. *Pediatric Exercise Science, 3*(4), 310–326.

Howard, Theresa Ruth (2019). *Keynote: Examining the difference between exposure, access and opportunity and how race, class, and the value systems of various culture groups affects ballet education.* Royal Opera House Young Talent Festival 2019 Symposium: Exposure, Access, and Opportunity: Exploring the Cultural Barriers to Ballet Training. 1st July 2019.

Issurin, V. B. (2017). Evidence-based prerequisites and precursors of athletic talent: a review. *Sports Medicine, 47*(10), 1993–2010.

Jackson, C. (1996). Managing and developing a boundaryless career: Lessons from dance and drama. *European Journal of Work and Organizational Psychology, 5*(4), 617–628.

Jayanthi, N., Pinkham, C., Dugas, L., Patrick, B., & LaBella, C. (2013). Sports specialization in young athletes: evidence-based recommendations. *Sports health, 5*(3), 251–257.

Kamin, S., Richards, H., & Collins, D. (2007). Influences on the talent development process of non-classical musicians: Psychological, social and environmental influences. *Music Education Research, 9*(3), 449–468.

Kearney, P. E., & Hayes, P. R. (2018). Excelling at youth level in competitive track and field athletics is not a prerequisite for later success. *Journal of sports sciences, 36*(21), 2502–2509.

Keay, N. (2019). Hormones and Dance Performance. One Dance UK. https://nickykeayfitness.files.wordpress.com/2019/04/oduk_issue_6_p47_48.pdf.

Kerr, G., Krasnow, D., & Mainwaring, L. (1992). The nature of dance injuries. *Medical Problems of Performing Artists, 7,* 25–29.

Kessler, R. C., Berglund, P., Demler, O., Jin, R., Merikangas, K. R., & Walters, E. E. (2005). Lifetime prevalence and age-of-onset distributions of DSM-IV disorders in the National Comorbidity Survey Replication. *Archives of general psychiatry, 62*(6), 593–602.

Kim, H. K., & McKenry, P. C. (1998). Social networks and support: a comparison of African Americans, Asian Americans, Caucasians, and Hispanics. *Journal of Comparative Family Studies, 29*(2), 313–334.

Krasnow, D., & Chatfield, S. J. (2009). Development of the 'performance competence evaluation measure': assessing qualitative aspects of dance performance. *Journal of Dance Medicine & Science, 13*(4), 101–107.

Kurdek, L. A., & Sinclair, R. J. (2001). Predicting reading and mathematics achievement in fourth-grade children from kindergarten readiness scores. *Journal of Educational Psychology, 93*(3), 451.

Laws, H. (2005). *Fit to Dance 2 - Report of the second national inquiry into dancers' health and injury in the UK*. London, UK: Newgate Press.

BIBLIOGRAPHY

Lebrun, F., & Collins, D. (2017). Is elite sport (really) bad for you? Can we answer the question?. *Frontiers in psychology, 8*, 324.

Lee, S. A. (2001). Adolescent issues in a psychological approach to dancers. *Journal of Dance Medicine & Science, 5*(4), 121–126.

Liefeith, A., Kiely, J., Collins, D., & Richards, J. (2018). Back to the Future – in support of a renewed emphasis on generic agility training within sports-specific developmental pathways. *Journal of sports sciences, 36*(19), 2250–2255.

Mackrell, J. (2015, April 13). Are British dancers really outclassed on the world stage? *The Guardian.* Retrieved from https://www.theguardian.com/stage/dance-blog/2015/apr/13/are-british-dancers-outclassed-on-the-world-stage-akram-khan-hofesh-schechter-lloyd-newson.

MacNamara, Á., & Collins, D. (2014). Staying with the 'force' and countering the 'dark side': Profiling, exploiting and countering psychological characteristics in talent identification and development. *The Sport Psychologist, 29*(1), 73–81.

MacNamara, Á., & Collins, D. (2017). Psychological characteristics of developing excellence: An educationally sound approach to talent development. In *Sport Psychology for Young Athletes* (pp. 116–128). Routledge.

MacNamara, Á., Button, A., & Collins, D. (2010). The role of psychological characteristics in facilitating the pathway to elite performance part 2: Examining environmental and stage-related differences in skills and behaviors. *The sport psychologist, 24*(1), 74–96.

MacNamara, Á., Button, A., & Collins, D. (2010). The role of psychological characteristics in facilitating the pathway to elite performance part 1: Identifying mental skills and behaviors. *The sport psychologist, 24*(1), 52–73.

MacPhee, D., Fritz, J., & Miller-Heyl, J. (1996). Ethnic variations in personal social networks and parenting. *Child development, 67*(6), 3278–3295.

Mainwaring, L., Kerr, G., & Krasnow, D. (1993). Psychological correlates of dance injuries. *Medical Problems of Performing Artists,* 8, 3–3.

Martindale, A., & Collins, D. (2005). Professional judgment and decision making: The role of intention for impact. *The Sport Psychologist, 19*(3), 303–317.

Maslow, A. (1966). *The Psychology of Science.*

Mitchell, S. (2017a). The growing dancer: Physiological challenges. One Dance UK Information Sheet.

Mitchell, S. (2017b). The growing dancer: Psychological challenges. One Dance UK Information Sheet.

Mitchell, S. B., Haase, A. M., Cumming, S. P., & Malina, R. M. (2017). Understanding growth and maturation in the context of ballet: a biocultural approach. *Research in Dance Education, 18*(3), 291–300.

Miulli, M., & Nordin-Bates, S. M. (2011). *Motivational climates: what they are, and why they matter.* IADMS Bull. Teach. 3, 5–7.

Murphy, G. M., Petitpas, A. J., & Brewer, B. W. (1996). Identity foreclosure, athletic identity, and career maturity in intercollegiate athletes. *The sport psychologist, 10*(3), 239–246.

Nordin-Bates, S.M. (2014). *Perfectionism.* Resource Paper. International Association for Dance Medicine and Science.

BIBLIOGRAPHY

Oreck, B. A., Owen, S. V., & Baum, S. M. (2003). Validity, reliability, and equity issues in an observational talent assessment process in the performing arts. *Journal for the Education of the Gifted, 27*(1), 62–94.

Orlick, T., & Partington, J. (1988). Mental links to excellence. *The sport psychologist, 2*(2), 105–130.

Pecen, E., Collins, D. J., & MacNamara, Á. (2018). 'It's your problem. Deal with it.' Performers' experiences of psychological challenges in music. *Frontiers in psychology, 8*, 2374.

Pecen, E., Collins, D., & MacNamara, Á. (2016). Music of the night: Performance practitioner considerations for enhancement work in music. *Sport, Exercise, and Performance Psychology, 5*(4), 377.

Persaud, R. (1997). *Staying Sane: How to Make Your Mind Work for You*. London: Bantam.

Pickard, A. (2007). 'My hobby has become my ambition': motivating factors from the perspective of young talented dancers. Paper presented at the From Cognition to Conditioning: the One-day UK Dance Science Forum, 19 February, in London, England.MacPhee, Fritz, and Miller-Hyel, 1996;.

Quested, E., & Duda, J. L. (2009). Perceptions of the motivational climate, need satisfaction, and indices of well-and ill-being among hip hop dancers. *Journal of Dance Medicine & Science, 13*(1), 10–19.

Quested, E., & Duda, J. L. (2010). Exploring the social-environmental determinants of well-and ill-being in dancers: A test of basic needs theory. *Journal of Sport and Exercise Psychology, 32*(1), 39–60.

Rafferty, S., & Wyon, M. (2006). Leadership behavior in dance application of the leadership scale for sports to dance technique teaching. *Journal of Dance Medicine & Science, 10*(1–2), 6–13.

Redding, E., Nordin-Bates, S. M., & Walker, I. J. (2011). Passion, Pathways and Potential in Dance: Trinity Laban Research Report: An interdisciplinary longitudinal study into dance talent development.

Rees, T., Hardy, L., Abernathy, B., Gullich, A., Côté, J., & Woodman, T. (2013). The UK Sport white paper: a systematic review of research into the identification and development of the world's best talent. *UK Sport*.

Rees, T., Hardy, L., Güllich, A., Abernethy, B., Côté, J., Woodman, T., & Warr, C. (2016). The great British medalists project: a review of current knowledge on the development of the world's best sporting talent. *Sports Medicine, 46*(8), 1041–1058.

Rigoli, D., Piek, J. P., Kane, R., & Oosterlaan, J. (2012). Motor coordination, working memory, and academic achievement in a normative adolescent sample: Testing a mediation model. *Archives of clinical neuropsychology, 27*(7), 766–780.

Risner, D. (2010). Dance education matters: Rebuilding postsecondary dance education for twenty-first century relevance and resonance. *Journal of Dance Education, 10*(4), 95–110.

Rose, M. S., Emery, C. A., & Meeuwisse, W. H. (2008). Sociodemographic predictors of sport injury in adolescents. *Medicine and science in sports and exercise, 40*(3), 444–450.

Sagan, C. (1995). *Demon-Haunted World: Science as a Candle in the Dark*. New York, NY: Random House.

Sarkisian, N., & Gerstel, N. (2004). Kin support among Blacks and Whites: Race and family organization. *American Sociological Review, 69*(6), 812–837.

BIBLIOGRAPHY

Savage, J., Collins, D., & Cruickshank, A. (2017). Exploring traumas in the development of talent: what are they, what do they do, and what do they require?. *Journal of Applied Sport Psychology*, 29(1), 101–117.

Schön, D. *The reflective practitioner: How practitioners think in action*. (San Francisco: Harper Collins, 1983).

Seligman, M. (2018). PERMA and the building blocks of well-being. *The Journal of Positive Psychology*, 13(4), 333–335.

Seligman, M.E.P. (1991). *Learned optimism*, New York: Vintage.

Seligman, M.E.P. (2011). *Flourish: A Visionary New Understanding of Happiness and Well-being*. New York: Free Press.

Simonton, D. (1999). Talent and its development: an emergenic and epigenetic model. *Psychological Review*, 106, 435–457.

Sloboda, J. A. (2000). *Musical performance and emotion: issues and developments, in Music, Mind and Science*, ed S. W. Yi (Seoul: Western Music Research Institute), 220–238.

Solomon, R., Solomon, J. (Eds.). (2017). *Dance Medicine & Science Bibliography*, Seventh Edition. Andover, NJ: J. Michael Ryan Publishing.

Subotnik, R. F., & Olszewski-Kubilius, P. (1997). Restructuring special programs to reflect the distinctions between children's and adults' experiences with giftedness. *Peabody Journal of Education*, 72(3–4), 101–116.

Subotnik, R. F., Olszewski-Kubilius, P., & Arnold, K.D. (2003). Beyond Bloom: Revisiting environmental factors that enhance or impede talent development. In J. H. Borland (Ed.), *Rethinking gifted education: Education and psychology of the gifted series* (pp. 227–238). New York: Teachers College Press.

Toering, T. T., Elferink-Gemser, M. T., Jordet, G., & Visscher, C. (2009). Self-regulation and performance level of elite and non-elite youth soccer players. *Journal of sports sciences*, 27(14), 1509–1517.

Thomas, H., & Tarr, J. (2009). Dancers' perceptions of pain and injury: positive and negative effects. *Journal of Dance Medicine & Science*, 13(2), 51–59.

Thomson, P., & Jaque, S. V. (2018). Childhood adversity and the creative experience in adult professional performing artists. *Frontiers in Psychology*, 9, 111.

Turney, K., & Kao, G. (2009). Assessing the private safety net: Social support among minority immigrant parents. *The Sociological Quarterly*, 50(4), 666–692.

Urmston, E. (2015). *Keeping the enjoyment alive: Positive psychology for dance*.

Vaeyens, R., Güllich, A., Warr, C. R., & Philippaerts, R. (2009). Talent identification and promotion programmes of Olympic athletes. *Journal of sports sciences*, 27(13), 1367–1380.Valkenburg, P. M., Koutamanis, M., & Vossen, H. G. (2017). The concurrent and longitudinal relationships between adolescents' use of social network sites and their social self-esteem. *Computers in human behavior*, 76, 35–41.

Vallerand, R. J., Paquet, Y., Philippe, F. L., & Charest, J. (2010). On the role of passion for work in burnout: A process model. *Journal of personality*, 78(1), 289–312.

van Rossum, J. H. (2001). Talented in dance: The Bloom stage model revisited in the personal histories of dance students. *High Ability Studies*, 12(2), 181–197.

Vardanis, F., Hopkins, R., Smith, K (creators). (2004–2020). Strictly Come Dancing. London, United Kingdom: BBC One.

BIBLIOGRAPHY

Vygotsky, L. S. (1978). *Mind in society: The development of higher psychological processes* (M. Cole, V. John-Steiner, S. Scribner & E. Souberman., Eds.) (A. R. Luria, M. Lopez-Morillas & M. Cole [with J. V. Wertsch], Trans.) Cambridge, Mass.: Harvard University Press. (Original manuscripts [ca. 1930-1934]).

Vygotsky, L. S. (1987). *Thinking and speech. The collected works of LS Vygotsky*, 1, 39–285.

Walker, I. J., Nordin-Bates, S. M., & Redding, E. (2010). Talent identification and development in dance: A review of the literature. *Research in Dance Education*, 11(3), 167–191.

Walker, I. J., Nordin-Bates, S. M., & Redding, E. (2011). Characteristics of talented dancers and age group differences: findings from the UK Centres for Advanced Training. *High Ability Studies*, 22(1), 43–60.

Wilson, G. D. (2002). *Psychology for performing artists* (2nd ed.). Philadelphia, PA, US: Whurr Publishers.

Wulff, H. (2020). *Ballet across borders: Career and culture in the world of dancers*. Routledge.

Zhou, M. (1997). Growing up American: The challenge confronting immigrant children and children of immigrants. *Annual review of sociology*, 23(1), 63–95.

Zimmerman, B. J. (2006). Development and adaptation of expertise: The role of self-regulatory processes and beliefs. *The Cambridge handbook of expertise and expert performance*, 186, 705–722.

ABOUT THE AUTHORS

DAVE COLLINS

Dave has over 350 peer-review publications and sixty books/chapters. Research interests include performer/coach development, expertise and peak performance. Dave holds certifications from the BPS, BASES and HCPC, plus professional qualifications in Teaching and Strength and Conditioning.

As a psychologist, he has worked with over seventy World or Olympic medallists plus professional teams and performers. Previously, as PD of UK Athletics, Dave directed the programme that progressed the team from 24th to 5th (World then Olympic) 21st to 3rd (World Indoors) and 12th to 1st (European Team). The established medal haul of eight at the Beijing Olympics makes Dave one of the most successful PD of recent times.

Current applied assignments include football, rugby, ski and snowboard and motorsport, plus work with non-sports organizations. Past attendance at eleven Olympics plus numerous World and European Championships and professional sports have provided useful experiences!

Dave has coached to national level in three sports, he is a fifth Dan Karate, Director of the Rugby Coaches Association and iZone Performance, Fellow of the Society of Martial Arts, ZSL and BASES, Associate Fellow of the BPS, and experienced PE teacher/teacher educator and an ex-Royal Marine.

ÁINE MACNAMARA

Áine's background is in physical education and coaching. She has worked with young people in a range of sporting environments as an educator, coach and sports psychology consultant. Her main research interest is in Talent Development and she has published widely, including over forty-five peer-review journals, fifteen book chapters and technical reports, and two books.

Áine has consulted with a range of sporting organizations in the UK and Ireland, including the FA, GAA, England Golf, Munster Rugby and Leinster GAA, helping them develop Talent Development pathways and policies, as well as providing coach and parent education to support the implementation of these ideas. Áine has been an invited speaker at national and international conferences and workshops focused on talent development, sport performance, youth sport and physical education, engaging frequently with NGBs of sport by contributing to coach education and player development workshops.

ERIN SANCHEZ

Erin Sanchez is an advocate, educator and applied researcher in dancers' health. She collaborates with colleagues in a variety of roles to support the mental and physical health of

ABOUT THE AUTHORS

dancers. Erin currently leads One Dance UK's Healthier Dancer Programme to empower the dance workforce to have sustainable and highly valued careers and to implement strategic objectives to improve dancers' health, wellbeing and performance. As manager of the National Institute of Dance Medicine and Science (NIDMS) she is also currently charged with ensuring a long-term future for NIDMS as a focal point to access dance medicine and science expertise, information and resources, and providing wider access for dancers across the UK to specialist, multidisciplinary, freely/easily accessible, preventative and rehabilitative physical and mental healthcare and performance enhancement. As a Registered Provider and Quality Assessor for Safe in Dance International, she leads international courses and assesses submissions in safe dance practice at UK level 6. She also manages an international group of teachers, dancers, and mental healthcare professionals and researchers, the Dance Psychology Network.

Erin is a member of the International Association for Dance Medicine and Science (www.iadms.org) and holds the qualification in Safe and Effective Dance Practice. She is pursuing her PhD in Sport, Physical Education, and Health Sciences from the University of Edinburgh and holds an MSc in Dance Science from Trinity Laban Conservatoire of Music and Dance and a BA (Hons) in Dance and Sociology from the University of New Mexico.

INDEX

mental welfare support 91–8
   challenging 91–2
   positive thinking 92–6
   preparation 90–1
mindsets, fixed and growth 38, 103
   developing 40
motor coordination & ability 57–8, 61–2
movement competence, actual 57–8
movement competence, basic 20
movement competence, perceived 59
multidisciplinary teams 83
nature vs nurture 36–8
nested practice approach 14, 76, 90, 91, 97
obsessive behaviour 80, 88, 100, 105, 106–7 see also maladaptive behaviour
Occam's Razor 127
over-persistence 40
parents & parenting 48, 87ff, 106–7, 113–14, 121
   sources of information for 121–3
passion, harmonious/obsessive 105–6
peak height velocity (PHV) 62
peer encouragement 76
perfectionism 15, 28, 29, 80, 97, 100, 103–5, 108, 111, 115, 117
   'reasonable' 29, 97
performance, determinants of 36
personally referenced excellence (PRE) 19, 24
physical literacy triangle 56, 57
physical self worth (PSW) 20, 22–3
positive attitude, instilling 40
positive thinking 92–6

praise and reward 40
pre-performance routine (PPR) 29
Professional Judgement & Decision-Making (PJDM) 28–9
Psychological Characteristics of Developing Excellence (PCDEs) 14, 29, 41–9, 88, 94, 103, 113, 114
relative energy deficit 11
self-evaluation 31
self-experimentation 27–9
self-regulation 13, 28, 36, 39, 45, 47–50, 109–10
skill refinement 65
social media, caution with 121–3
specialization, early vs general 60–2
styles of dance, experiences of 28
super-compensation 66
talent, as a developmental construct 36–8
talent, multiplicative components 37–8
talent, seen as a gift 36, 39
talent development process (TD) 71–84
   formal training, considerations 81–2
   leadership 83
   physical environment 84
   positive environments 83–4
   possible negative outcomes 82
   skillsets 83–4
   training environment 83
   varied professional pathways 81
talent identification (TI), factors in 73ff
   age 73–4
   chance 74
   economic means 76–7

INDEX

    genetics 73
    genres 74
    peer encouragement 76
    race/ethnicity 77
    society/cultural environment 74–6
talent vs success 82
teach-test-tweak-repeat cycle 45–6, 51, 91, 92
Tharp, Kenneth 13
training, experienced body 66–67
weight issues 11, 100, 110
zone of proximal development 48–9